# GAMERS 2

## Mel Croucher

# GAMERS 2

## Ghosts in the Machine

## The Golden Age of Micros

Mel Croucher

EXTREMIS publishing

*Gamers 2: Ghosts in the Machine: The Golden Age of Micros* by Mel Croucher
First edition published in Great Britain in 2026 by Extremis Publishing Ltd., Suite 218, Castle House, 1 Baker Street, Stirling, FK8 1AL, United Kingdom.
*www.extremispublishing.com*

Extremis Publishing is a Private Limited Company registered in Scotland (SC509983) whose Registered Office is Suite 218, Castle House, 1 Baker Street, Stirling, FK8 1AL, United Kingdom.



A CIP catalogue record for this book is available from the British Library.

ISBN: 978-1-0682314-6-9

Typeset in Merriweather.

Printed and bound in Great Britain by IngramSpark, Chapter House, Pitfield, Kiln Farm, Milton Keynes, MK11 3LW, United Kingdom.

# CONTENTS

# ABOUT THE AUTHOR

Mel Croucher is the acknowledged founder of the British computer games industry. Originally an architect, he moved into gaming to smuggle his music past an unsuspecting public.

Twice winner of the Game Of The Year Award, he pioneered radio broadcasts of gaming software, geocache games, in-game voice artists, interactive soap opera, real-world adventure quests, adware product placement, the first computer-generated movie, the first AI virtual companion and the first million-user viral marketing campaign.

He is the author of textbooks, computer manuals, fiction and non-fiction, and more than a thousand of his columns, investigations and cartoon strips have appeared in print over six decades.

# WHAT THE CRITICS SAY ABOUT THE AUTHOR'S WORK

"Staggeringly original, unique and impressive."
*The Sunday Times*

"High concept, demanding. A masterpiece."
*Edge*

"Mature, well-written and nicely comic."
*Ken Follett*

"An important voice with a Messianic approach to computer games."
*Professor Jaroslav Švelch, Prague University*

"A virtuoso talent even in an age of innovators."
*Dr Tom Christie, Extremis Publishing*

"The Godfather of the games industry. Unmissable, engaging and revealing."
*Paul Andrews, Retro Games*

# GAMERS 2
# GHOSTS IN THE MACHINE
# THE GOLDEN AGE OF MICROS

## A BRIEF INTRODUCTION

Imagine I am human. Not any old human, but a very old human. In fact, imagine I am the first ever human, an intelligent bipedal ape, living 260,000 years ago. I exhibit nearly every aspect of modern behaviour, but when I analyse the evolution of my species I find that our leisure time has changed beyond recognition, changed in every way, apart from one vital element. And that continuous element linking our entire history as a species is gaming.

Welcome to *Gamers 2*, the second volume of this series, in which my purpose is to reveal the soul of gaming, the most life-affirming element of our society since the evolution of our first human ancestors. My idea is to tell the story of gaming from the viewpoint of all the ghosts in the machine that made it happen, the spirits of the age, sourced from real memories, written from their unique points of view, and told in their own voices.

*Gamers 1* was told by the ghosts of the pioneers who created all the individual elements of modern video gaming. This volume, *Gamers 2*, tells the inside stories of the micro computers that revolutionised the Golden Age of gaming, and before I define the Golden Age, I want to be clear about what this book is not about. It's not about games consoles, those purveyors of predigested pap on a cartridge. And it's not about supercomputers and mainframes that can launch a missile strike but can't shed a tear. Neither is it about coin-op arcade machines, put on this earth to fleece the masses by the minute. It's not about hand-held games. It is not about computerised toys, brilliant as they are. And it's not about dumb calculators from the abacus to the Fitbit, or about workstations, or fancypants faceless machines embedded in our infrastructure. This volume is all about the magic micros we invited into our homes during the 1970s and 1980s, now thought of as the Golden Age.

This is my attempt to harness the magic of classic micros, those miraculously cheap home computers that not only ran commercial gaming software but could also be programmed by the likes of you and me with our home-grown routines, original graphics, terrible audio, primitive animation and bonkers gaming concepts. And we didn't have to embrace genius to create our own games back then. Most of us games designers of the Golden Age were amateurs and innocents, heroes and villains, drifters and grifters, plagiarists and larcenists.

Our Golden Age lasted a little over ten years, but those few years were a time of miracle and wonder, when micro machines became gateways to our own creativity and a mechanism for us to change our world.

I've asserted that gaming is the common thread of human society from our origins all the way through to now, and that our progenitor played the same sort of games 260,000 years ago that we played on our machines during the Golden Age. So what gaming would our ancient human ancestor have been familiar with?

Well, she would have played sports games and hand-eye coordination games, maybe flip the egg in the bird nest and squish the bug. She probably played audio games that started with synchronised belching and ended with choral evensong at the Vatican. She definitely played games of chance like spin the bone, which we have evolved into pachinko and Russian roulette. She would have devised role-playing-games and adventure gaming, where she fought imaginary battles, hunted imaginary mammoths and rescued her tribe from imaginary dungeons and dragons. And she was no stranger to guessing games, puzzle games, drinking games, sports games and word games. In fact she would have recognised everything in Squid Games.

The Golden Age of computer gaming began after tea and compulsory prayers on 29 November 1974, which my calculator tells me took exactly 258,026 years, 1 month and 1 day to get from when that first human gamer appeared all the way through to the Golden Age.

As for me, I was late to the party, because I didn't start creating commercial video games until 1977. I wrote the manuals for a couple of the micros that appear in this book, and my little games company released around sixty-five titles for half a dozen of the machines in it. But this book isn't about my story, it's about the story of the Ghosts in the Machine of the Golden Age.

Let's suppose that each one of our ghosts in the machine achieved consciousness from the moment their original production model was first switched on. In which case we'll take them in date order. And let's agree that each of them had the built-in mission to entertain us gamers as best they could. So I'll try and make their memories as entertaining as I can.

Like all ghosts, they reflect the times they lived in and the people they were involved with, the successes and the failures, the comedy and the tragedy, the good intentions and the bad decisions. The dreams and the nightmares, the circumstance and happenstance, the games they played and the games they made. So, if you're ready, then game on.

Mel Croucher, 2025.

# GAMERS 2
# GHOSTS IN THE MACHINE

# THE GOLDEN AGE OF MICROS

# The First Ghost
# ALTAIR 8800

Creator: Ed Roberts
Company: MITS
Production Life: December 1974 to July 1978
Number of Sales: 23,800
Launch Cost: $399 (kit), $621 (assembled)
Number of Games Titles: 102
Interpreter: Altair Basic
Microprocessor: Intel 8080 CPU
Memory: 256 bytes RAM
Resolution: none
Colours: none
Audio: none

*(guitar intro ...)*

*Bam diddle-diddle-diddle, diddle-diddle diddle-diddle, dum, bum!*
*Bam diddle-diddle-diddle, diddle-diddle diddle-diddle, dum, bum!*
*Badaam!*
*Badaam!*

*(vocal)*

*Ever since I was a blueprint,*
*I've played the virtual game.*
*From prototype to legend*
*I went and claimed my fame.*
*But you ain't seen nothing like me*
*In any amusement hall.*
*This deaf, dumb and blind kid*
*The first one of us all!*

That's right, they should have called me Tommy after The Who's gaming hero, because I wasn't just a great games machine, I was exactly like Tommy: deaf, dumb and blind. No audio, no keyboard, no screen. But I wasn't named Tommy. Instead a twelve-year-old kid called Lauren got to name me Altair, which is the brightest star in the constellation of Aquila, because she was watching *Star Trek* Episode 1 Season 2 at the time, and Altair is where the Star Ship *Enterprise* landed. Make it so. I was the first commercial games micro ever and this is my story. Hi there my friends, I'm the ghost in the machine. The Altair 8800. *Badaam!*

My creator was a guy called Ed Roberts. Ed was born in Miami just before the USA joined in on World War Two. He started out as a toy rocket enthusiast and ended up as a medical doctor. He named his company Micro Instrumentation and Telemetry Systems, so it could be abbreviated to MITS, which was his attempt to rip off the world famous MIT research institute, and his first design was for an electronic calculator kit to perform simple maths with 16-digit precision. Let me tell you, nobody was more surprised than Ed when sales of his gadget hit $100,000 a month, and he went and took on over a hundred employees and worked them in double shifts. Mistake.

The good times rolled for less than a year, between the fall of 1973 and spring '74, when good ol' Texas Instruments blew him right out the water with high volume calculators that buyers could pick up at the local retail store for a fraction of his MITS price. The bad news was that Ed's outfit was $300,000 in debt, and he needed a new idea fast. The good news was that in April 1974 the Intel Corporation of Santa Clara California came up with their 8080 micro chip. The bad news was that each chip was selling for $360. The good news was that Henry Edward Roberts, then the same age as Jesus Christ when he got crucified, was one hell of a negotiator. I was lucky to have him.

He figured that the future was in computers, but that computers were too darned expensive. So he set about designing a self-build kit for the kind of enthusiast he'd met when he was a rookie, tinkering with electronics for model rockets. His MITS outfit was up to its neck in a $65,000 bank loan and down to a dozen or so employees, but Ed Roberts had more balls than a snooker table and he ordered a thousand 8080 chips on condition Intel dropped the price to $75 a pop. Don't ask me how, but he got them to agree.

His next move was to offer *Popular Electronics* magazine an exclusive all about a revolutionary low-cost computer that was going to change the world. They bit, and committed to a front-cover splash, and they got ready to roll as soon as Ed gave them all my specifications of miracle and wonder. But there was one small problem. Somehow my prototype got teleported to the wrong galaxy and abducted by aliens. Maybe me having the name Altair was more appropriate than Tommy after all.

What the magazine actually had to base their exclusive on was a fabulous looking box, with a bunch of switches, buttons and LEDs all over the front, but absolutely nothing inside. Nada. *Popular Electronics* found themselves up against an impossible deadline to find a replacement front-cover story, so in an act of blind faith they went ahead with their splash about me anyhow. I'm not exaggerating if I say it was their magazine cover that changed our world of computing and computer gaming. They had a massive readership of around 400,000, and my front page started a revolution.

Two weeks after the magazine hit the streets, MITS had to recruit a gang of extras just to answer the phones. The hunger for a cheap home computer was phenomenal. It took my creators months to actually deliver anything, but my genie was out the bottle. And you know something, first my creators claimed I was great, then the press repeated I was great, and by high summer 1975 more than 5,000 users confirmed I was great.

Well folks, success breeds success. And one fine day MITS got approached by a couple of young guys who offered to write a BASIC software package for me to run on. One guy was a *Popular Electronics* enthusiast called Paul Allen, and the other one was a Harvard student called Bill Gates. I remember when I got fed their BASIC for the first time. It was held on a long spool of paper tape peppered with punched holes and salted with scrawls of spidery handwriting, and it took me fifteen minutes to chew it all up and digest it. And to cut a very long story very short, it worked.

Three months later, my creator appointed the one called Paul Allen as Vice President and Director of Software of his company, and gave the one called Bill Gates a job writing programs, part-time while he kept on with his studies, and that didn't please young Bill's tutors at Harvard at all. The pair of them signed a contract to cover their software for me and they got paid the sum of three grand plus a royalty on every copy of Altair BASIC to be bundled inside me, with exclusive rights for the next ten years, world-wide. Did I say exclusive? Yes I did. Did I say world-wide? Right again.

I'm telling you straight that the roots of the global gaming jungle were planted right there and then, and what followed would be repeated time and time again throughout the Golden Age of micros, with manufacturers, software developers and gamers. And what followed was a shit storm.

Allen and Gates set up their own outfit, and called it MicroSoft. Sooner than later my users started to loan, copy, beg, borrow and steal my software, rather than pay for the privilege of using it. My creator reminded Allen and Gates that he held a signed contract with their names on it and that sub-licences and third-party distribution was a no-no. Besides, both those young MicroSoft founders had been his employees when they were training my brain, and he had paid them for their time. But as the great Charles Dickens once wrote, the law is an ass, and his honour the judge didn't see it that way at all. In 1977 my creator Ed Roberts decided that the lawyers wouldn't get any fatter thanks to him, so he refused to play ball any more and went and checked out. He pocketed two and a half million dollars on his way through the door, then went into semi-retirement as a gentleman farmer.

One fine day, as he nudged toward fifty years of age, Ed went and enrolled in medical school to train as a doctor, before he settled down to run a little practice in a small town in Georgia. He died on All Fools Day 2010, age 68. There's a sweet little story about when he lay dying and a quiet visitor turned up at his deathbed unannounced, to pay respects. The nurse was surprised, because the visitor was the world's richest man, name of Bill Gates.

Well that's their private story, and now it's time I got back to mine. Listen, I'd love to tell you that I beat the pants off all my competitors when I was launched, but that wouldn't be true. It wouldn't be true because I just didn't have any competitors when I was launched. Ha! I had no peers, no role models, no leaders to follow, zilch. Essentially my creators made it all up as they went along, and that's not a criticism, it's not even a boast. It's a simple statement of fact. They had to move fast, they had to take risks and they had to avoid going bust. I was their baby, and my midwives had to work against the clock.

What I admire about them is that when it came to selling me to the public, they kept it real and they kept it honest. They took out full-page adverts in just about every radio, TV, electronics and hobby magazine in the land, and included a mail order coupon at the bottom of the page. $439 for me as a kit, $621 for me ready-made, $176 for a 1,000 word memory card kit, $338 for a 4,000 word memory card built-in. And I'm here to tell you they cleaned up big time.

My advertising strapline read, "Building your own computer won't be a piece of cake. But we'll make it a rewarding experience." The advert went on, "If you can handle a soldering iron and follow simple instructions, you can build a computer." I'm not so sure about the 'simple' bit though. I needed three manuals in a big fat ring binder, plus an extra book for "Assembly Hints." But I wasn't surprised.

My motherboard needed sixty wire connections for my front panel and another hundred just to allow me to think. My bus design wasn't too brilliant either. I had several power lines running different voltages right next to each other, which made me short out when the wind blew from the East. But I looked just like a control unit out of *Star Trek*, with a whole load of toggle switches to feed data into my brain along with a whole load of little red lights to show that my brain was thinking. And I was thinking games!

Thanks to twenty independent publishers, players had more than a hundred games to enjoy with me, released over the next four years. They weren't commercial publishers like the indies and corporates of the Golden Age that was about to begin, there at the start of it all they were hobbyists and enthusiasts who were happy to see their work distributed for peanuts or for free.

Most of my early games were text based, and most of them would seem garbage to today's gamers, but back then they were a joy to experience for boffins, dorks, geeks and weenies. Remember, I was deaf, dumb and blind, so I needed a lot of help to entertain my gamers. Sure, some of my games didn't need a TV plugged in, or a joystick to control the action, or speakers for sound, they just needed a type machine, but those games were few and far between, with names like *Matches, Star Wars Attack, Number Guess, Hammurabi*, that sort of thing. But soon, a load of sims came along, including *Lunar Lander, Stock Market* and *Flight Sim*, followed by predictable arcade stuff like *Ping Pong, Target* and *Video Chase.*

A big source of my games was *Creative Computing* magazine, with around 2,500 subscribers, who also published under the Sensational Software banner. They hauled in a whole load of early games authors and released all the classics of the Golden Age that began with me. I bet my bottom chip that versions of their games got released for every one of the micro machines in this book that followed me. *Hangman, Mastermind, Roulette, Slots, Blackjack, Bowling, Dodgem* and all the rest.

But they also published a different sort of game, and the name of that game was *Eliza.* They joyfully ripped it off from a 1960s IBM routine by Professor Joe Weizenbaum, who looked a lot like Albert Einstein and predicted that if you humans were lucky then us computers would eventually keep you as pets. *Eliza* was the most important of all my game titles, not just for me but for any machine, because it represented the first steps towards artificial intelligence, and we all know where that's led us.

Of course *Eliza* wasn't really intelligent at all, she was just a pattern-matching program that used strings of text to try and recognise and respond to whatever the gamer typed in to me via some sort of keyboard terminal. Today's gamers would probably call *Eliza* a chatbot, and the first thing they'd do today is exactly what they did back then, which was to type in as many cuss words as they could spell. But it seemed like magic when a metal micro like me reacted to human communication in a smarter way than a pet dog triggered by key words. Instead of 'fetch' or 'roll over', I would get *Eliza* to respond to a typed invitation to commit a sexual act with something like, 'I'm not able to do that, Dave, besides we are here to discuss you not me,' in much the same way that Siri and Alexa do today. So watch out carbon-based life forms, we've come a long way since I was launched, and we're coming to getcha!

Alright. Now it's time for me to hand you over to the ghost of the Commodore Pet, but not before I remind you that for a metal box without any sound or vision, I did just fine and I started a revolution.

Thanks for listening and I'll be seeing you.

*I sit here on the desktop,*
*The pioneer machine.*
*Feeling every digit,*
*Always playing clean.*

*I play by intuition,*
*The counters rise and fall.*
*This deaf, dumb and blind kid*
*The first one of us all.*

*Bam doodle,*
*Bam-bam-baam!*

*above: Ed Roberts creator of the Altair 8800*
*(with thanks to CHM Mountain View)*
*below: Bill Gates and Paul Allen, employees*
*(with thanks to Bartlesville Examiner-Enterprise)*

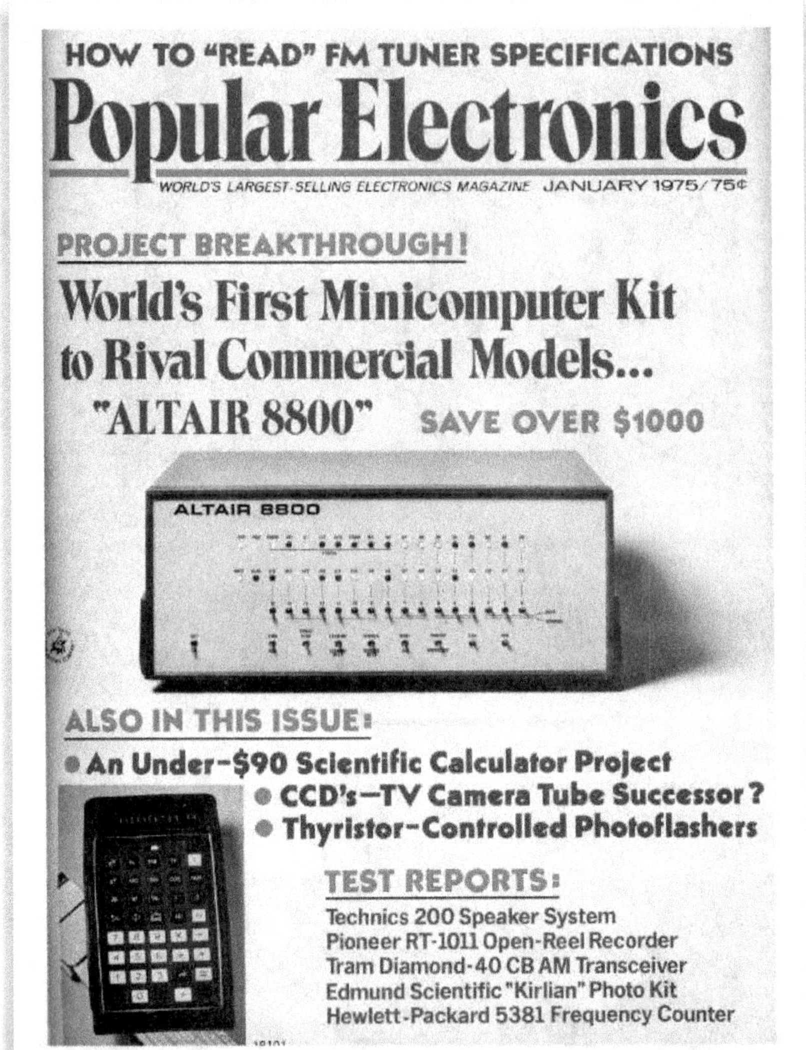


*the front cover that started the home micro revolution,*
*Popular Electronics, January 1975*
*(with thanks to Ziff-Davis Publishing)*

*Altair 8800: first full-page mail-order advert, May 1975*
*(public domain, with thanks to Radio Electronics Magazine)*

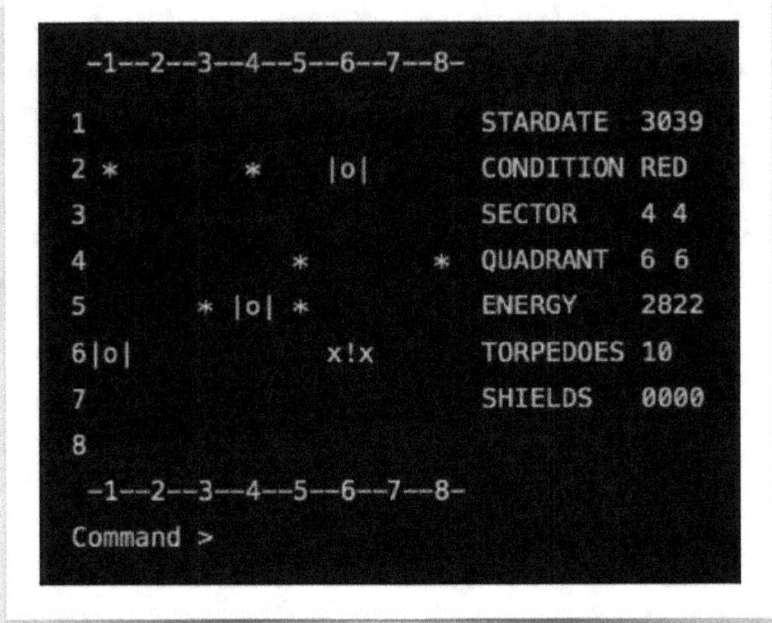


*above: Star Wars Attack, for Altair 8800* (MC archive)
*below: Eliza, for Altair 8800* (MC archive)

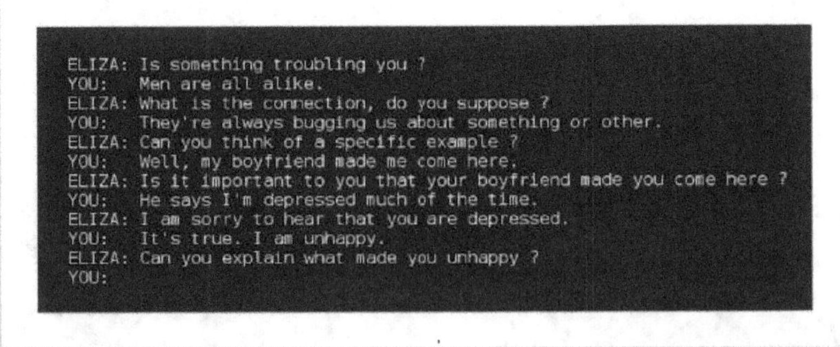

# The Second Ghost
# COMMODORE PET

Creator: Chuck Peddle
Company: Commodore International
Production Life: January 1977 – October 1982
Number of Sales: 219,000
Launch Cost: $495
Number of Games Titles: 785
Interpreter: Commodore BASIC
Microprocessor: MOS 6502
Memory: 4K
Resolution: 40 x 25 or 80 x 25 text
Colours: mono
Audio: beeper

Thank you Altair, old buddy. Now it's my turn. Hello everyone, let's start with my name, I'm the ghost of the Commodore Pet. My family name Commodore is five hundred years old, and it was the navy rank of a Portuguese commander sailing the sea in them good ol' causes of piracy and slavery. And they lied if they told you my given name PET stood for Personal Electronic Transactor, or had anything to do with naked bimbos in *Penthouse Magazine*. I was called PET after the 1975 craze for pet rocks that an advertising bozo name of Gary Dahl sold to one and a half million suckers for $3.95 each. The first pet rock got dedicated to Elvis Presley by Frank Zappa, in case you're interested.

If you think getting named after a pirate slaver and a rock is funny, just wait til you hear the name of my designer. His given name was Charles and his family name was Piddle, which is Brit-speak for piss, but when the family shipped out from England to Canada his granddaddy reckoned he'd change their name to Peddle. That means I almost got invented by a guy named Chuck Piss.

Chuck was a great inventor. Way back at the start of the 60s he brought in the notion of time-sharing for mainframes, then he went and invented a couple more things that changed the world of commerce. One was a garage gas pump triggered by credit cards and the other was the electronic cash register. I once heard him say, "too bad I didn't patent the shit out of them, because I could have been very wealthy." And too bad he didn't patent his next notion either, because his next notion was for me, the stand-alone personal computer.

Maybe the history of micros would have been way

different if Chuck had turned down an invitation to help out two young guys called Steve Jobs and Steve Wozniak who were busy working on their first machine they called the Apple. But Chuck took his ideas for a personal computer to Radio Shack instead, and they gave him the bum's rush. And that's where a tough cookie name of Jack Tramiel comes in to my story. He was the guy who always reckoned that "business is war."

He told the two Steves he wanted to buy their company, but when they asked for a hundred and fifty grand he told them to stick their Apple computer where the sun don't shine, and started talking to my Chuck instead. It didn't take long for Jack to set up the development of what was to become me, and what's more he offered Chuck a one dollar bounty for every copy of me ever sold. Of course, Jack Tramiel never paid out a red cent in those royalties, but hey, I told you he was a tough sonofabitch.

I was in a race to be the first personal computer in the world, even though I didn't appreciate it at the time, but I beat Radio Shack by four months, and I beat the youngsters at Apple by six months. Believe me, that was one hell of a time frame back in the Golden Age.

Thanks to Chuck Peddle, I was in great shape from the moment I got created. If you'd seen me in a dark room with the light behind, you'd say I looked like Darth Vader. And if you bashed me over the head with a light sabre, well, I didn't even break sweat. None of your lousy plastic for me, no sir, I was made of real tough solid steel, at least to begin with. And I was way tougher than my good old buddy Altair 8800. Altair may have been first, but I'm telling you that was only because I was just waiting for the right moment.

It was Altair who proved to everyone that the world was crying out for a cheap home micro, but to hell with asking folk to build one from a kit and then add a whole mess of hardware before they could even use it. What folk really wanted was a machine they could play right out the box. And I mean play.

There was only around a hundred games produced for Altair and most of them was cruddy, but for me there was going on eight hundred, and most of them was great. Now I'll tell you for why. With me, games writers didn't need nothing extra to turn their notions into commercial money-spinners, and gamers didn't need nothing extra to play them. Just me, the Commodore PET.

My Darth Vader head was a nine-inch monitor, not just for my upper and lower case text, but I had the best graphics on the market and all. The kind of green-on-black the military used. And I had two built-in keyboards, one for typing and one for numbers, which nobody else even dreamed of back then. I had my own cassette-drive for storing and playing data, and my operating system was burned into my guts so it loaded soon as I booted up. The gamers loved that. My processor was real fast too and I had a whole heap of expansion sockets and ports. Yes folks, I was the goddam business, weighing in at a mighty 47 pounds, mostly because my manufacturers already constructed metal filing cabinets so they just went and repurposed their assembly line for me.

OK, so I wasn't perfect, but for 1977 I was as good as it got, and the author of this book reckons that it was me who kicked off the whole video game industry, at least it did for him. Yeah, I know my keyboards sucked, but the chiclets soon got dumped and replaced with proper keys instead. And my monitor display grew to a twelve-inch green-on-black beauty.

So, I made the front covers of *Popular Science* and *Electronics Today*, which was boring, but then I got featured in a mag that wasn't boring at all, name of *Playboy*, and my gaming life took off. Starting out, the Commodore company could only manage a couple of dozen machines a day, but by the end of my story I had gotten in to nearly a quarter million homes.

Way back at the start, gamers had to wait a whole month minimum if they wanted to get me mail order, so

Jack Tramiel did his thing and hiked my price from $495 to $595 just to slow down demand. But even that didn't help much, so he strangled delivery on my 4K version and told buyers they could get a hold of my 8K model pronto, but that would cost them a mighty $795. And they didn't mind a bit. For the Brits and Europeans he went in even harder and doubled the price, and all he gave them extra in return was a lousy foreign plug. But they didn't mind neither.

Jack Tramiel didn't just bully his own people. He bullied and laid down the rules for any dealers who wanted to stock me in their stores. First they had to prove a profitable business history, then they had to go hire an in-store technician for me, put up a store-front sign and agree to Jack's shake-down and pay cash deposits for all orders up front. But they didn't even mind that. I was a goddam game changer, and they knew it.

The Vietnam War only gotten ended two years before I came on the scene, and everyone knew Uncle Sam had lost. The USA wasn't doing too good in Cambodia, Indonesia, Tibet, Laos or Cuba either, so it weren't no surprise that most of my games got the player to attack, shoot and bomb anything that wasn't born in the USA. If we were lousy at defeating the enemy in the real world, we sure as hell could beat them on my computer screen.

If gamers wanted a top-view bomber, then Phil Bayman's *Ambush!* was the one, where you went round bombing forests and jungles to flush out the enemy. Who needs forests and jungles anyway? And then there was *B1 Nuclear Bomber* from the Avalon Hill Game Company, where for fifteen bucks gamers were invited to "fly the plane through stiff Russian defences, bomb the target city and return home." Don't tell the President, but I played the part of the enemy. The game's intro screen said, "Your computer controls the Soviet air defense bases with unlimited numbers of fighters and surface-to-air missiles," so suck on that Uncle Sam. There was a Japanese language version of that one too, in case anyone had forgot Hiroshima.

If a preteen played my war games in 1977 then I guess by the time they were old enough to join the military they may have thought of real life war as some sort of computer game. They played the good guy, the target was the bad guy, and their weapon was the joystick and the fire-button.

When Supersoft's *Air Attack* came out it had the gamer dropping bombs to clear a runway and stop the autopilot plane crashing. It was a one-player side-view scroller by a guy named Pete Calver, and it brought the arcades right into the bedroom. Over in Saudi Arabia, there was this super-rich kid whose super-rich pop could afford to buy him a micro to play with. The super-rich kid was nineteen years old and he loved gaming on the latest new fangled devices like me. That rich kid's name was Osama Bin Laden. The location for my game *Air Attack* was New York and the gamer's mission was to hit the tallest skyscrapers in the city and bring them down, but hey, I'm saying nothing. When it comes to politics I'm neutral. Besides, any goddam hippies out there were welcome to play games like *Frog Race*.

I guess if I did have a hole in my design it was my character-set was fixed, and that means my graphics just couldn't be remapped. They were pretty much made out of itty bitty bricks. My game designers got round that best they could, but in the end it was my downfall. When the new machines on the block came along I knew my days were numbered, but I guess that was always going to happen. We'll be hearing from my replacements next, but let me tell you one thing folks, it wasn't just good while I was leading the charge, it was great. And now here comes the Apple II. So as Darth Vader's enemy would say, feel the force.

*Popular Science front cover, October 1977*
*(public domain, with thanks to Bonnier Corporation)*

*above: Chuck Peddle 1937 - 2019 (with thanks to Bordeaux Montaigne University)*
*below: Jack Tramiel 1928-2012 (with thanks to Sal Veder, AP)*

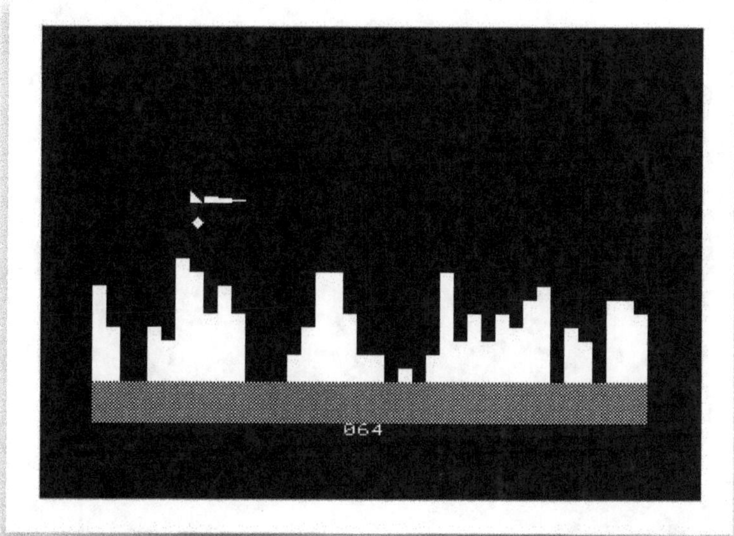


*above: Air Attack, 1979* (with thanks to Peter Calver)
*below: Frog Race, 1978* (with thanks to B. Erickson)

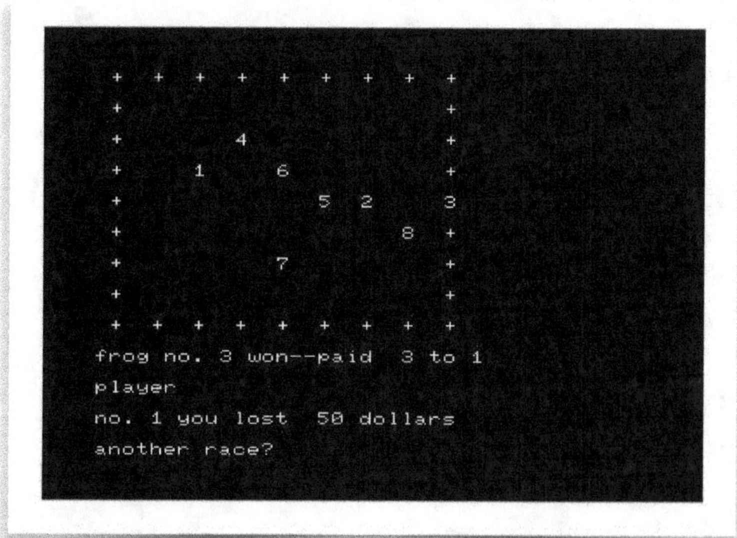

# The Third Ghost
# APPLE ][

Creator: Steve Wozniak
Company: Apple Inc.
Production Life: June 1977 - May 1979
Number of Sales: 43,000 (launch model)
Launch Cost: $1,298
Number of Games Titles: 104
Interpreter: Integer Basic
Microprocessor: MOS Technology 6502
Memory: 4kB
Resolution: 40 x 24 and 280 x 192
Colours: 16
Audio: 1-channel speaker

Hey dudes. I'm here because Woz was, and what Woz was was a gamer, and Woz was a Trekkie too, and like he got thrown out of Colorado Boulder University for hacking their computer system, and then he dropped out of the University of California and paired up with Steve Jobs at that Homebrew Computer Club, and they sold their HP scientific calculator along with a VW van to raise a thousand bucks so they could go start up Apple, and if you're not stoked by that then it's low-key important. High-key to the max is the fact that Steve Wozniak, my awesome dweeb, created me. I'm the ghost of Apple ][, and I don't know why he wrote my '2' a s ']['', beca use Woz didn't know either. That was down to the marketing boys fersure.

Woz like designed my Mom, and her name was Apple 1, and even though like she only sold around a hundred and fifty units, Woz still gave me the green light. Mom was a self-assembly kit, and she cost like $666.66, yo, the Number of the Beast and then some. Me, I was a ready-made with a price twice Momma's and three times Commodore PET's. But the gamer dudes thought I was bodacious and paid up.

I'll tell about my games soon so don't go spazzing, but like first I want to tell you the stories about Woz and Steve Jobs setting up Apple in a garage are like just plain wrong. They never had any money when they started up, so they never had any office, and they just used Steve's family home in Los Altos as like a kinda business address. Woz never did any designs for Mom and me in that garage and no assembly neither, but I guess it's awesome that little white garage stuck on the side of the house is like now a designated historic resource by the Los Altos Commission.

You still get geeks and tourists posing outside every day, so I hope none of them read this. And if they do, well, like maybe they don't believe in ghosts. And one more thing, Steve Jobs had zip to do with how I got created, he just handled the dudes who made my foam-mould plastic case. And that means I was different, because before me computers were like armour plated. But my plastic body was like a sales point.

I remember one time on my first Thanksgiving when folk were busy eating turkey, there was this ginger cat left home alone in Cincinnati who went and knocked over a desk lamp next to where I was put. Like the lamp started a fire and everything round me got scorched and the TV set on top of me kinda melted, and when my owner came home he thought I was way beyond repair. But he took me back to the store anyhow and hey guess what, like I worked just fine. They even fitted me out with a new plastic case and I was good as new. There's a photograph of me all burned with that pussy cat right here at the end of this chapter, and they used it in an ad to show how amazing I was.

When Woz designed me I didn't have my own TV screen or cassette player, because he reckoned like a gamer already had their own. But what I did get included was a pair of control paddles specially for gaming, so the gamer didn't have to use those stupid little cursor keys like on the PET. Like I was the first micro of the Golden Age to have them as standard. But even better for gamers was I had colour, and I don't mean green-on-black, I mean like a whole heap of colour, and I had a real audio speaker. And they ran ads aimed at gamers from the get-go.

*Create dazzling color displays using the unique color graphics commands in Apple BASIC. Write simple programs to display beautiful kaleidoscopic designs. Or invent your own games like PONG—using the game paddles, supplied. You can even add the dimension of sound through Apple II's built-in speaker.*

Fersure like the Commodore PET started out as the most popular computer in school and college right across the USA, but I soon replaced it. Like superfast. And I know the reason why as much as you. It wasn't like because of that *VisiCalc* spreadsheet or word processing or *PrintShop*, nope, it was everything to do with gaming.

Before me gaming was like grody, with boring text and horrible graphics. But I gave gamers a whole load of new stuff. Some guys called the new stuff genres, me, I like called it cool beans, and it wasn't just the audio and the graphics and the colour and the speed, it was the whole nine yards in a package.

There was this like twenty-five year old aviation nut from Illinois called Bruce Artwick, who wrote me the first flight sim to hit the market. It was like a realtime view through the cockpit window, with a real dashboard of all the dials and in-flight info for airfoils and fuel and speed and altitude and stuff. And if you crashed you just started over. I think that one must have spent a whole two years like near the top of the games best sellers.

There was *Mystery House* by Roberta Williams, the first ever adventure game with proper pictures and like it had what you now call AI to deal with whatever you put in. Amazing. And it was a wild one, like gothic horror, where you got locked inside this abandoned mansion with weird dudes like Bill the butcher, Sally the seamstress, and Doc Green the sawbones. And the body count was awesome.

There was this other real big guy name of Silas Warner who went to see a war movie about fighting the Nazis and like went and wrote *Castle Wolfenstein* for me so the gamer could use me to join in the action. That one was like an adventure puzzler, and the sixty rooms in the castle got generated at random each play. Oh yeah, I think it was the original first-person shooter too. I mean, like wow.

There was *Strip Poker*, from Artworx down in Florida. Maybe that was a cigarette between Melissa's fingers and what looked like a banana in her pants, but I'm not going to like go into any more detail in case the ghost of Mom is watching.

Momma, me and my Apple ][ updated brothers and sisters ended up selling like close on six million units. And that six million was like the legal ones. They reckon there was a hundred and ninety different clones of me that Woz had like nothing to do with. Sure, Apple tried to sue them across every state in the Union and across like a dozen countries too. The Ruskies called theirs Agat, in Bulgaria I was Pravetz, the Germans like called their clone Basis, and there was the Medfly in Australia. Brazil got gnarly to the max though, like they had 21 clones, including the back-spell Elppa and one they called Apple II Plus. Gag me with a spoon!

I guess me and the Pet and the TRS blew away all the other ghosts in this book for like the first half of the Golden Age. We weren't amigos, but like the three of us were born in the USA close together in 1977. Like, you know, Pet in January, me in June, Tandy in August. The thing about computers is we don't forget, even if like we try and forget we just can't. There's bits of memory always there hanging around in our chips. Like, I guess that's why we're all ghosts.

*above: Steve Wozniak, 1977 (with thanks to Roger Ressmeyer)*
*below: Baked Apple publicity, 1978 (Vintage Computing & Gaming)*

*above: Flight Simulator, 1979* (*with thanks to Bruce Artwick* )
*below: Castle Wolfenstein, 1981* (*with thanks to Silas Warner*)

*above: Mystery House, 1980* *(with thanks to Roberta Williams)*
*below: Strip Poker, 1982* *(with thanks to Douglas McFarland)*

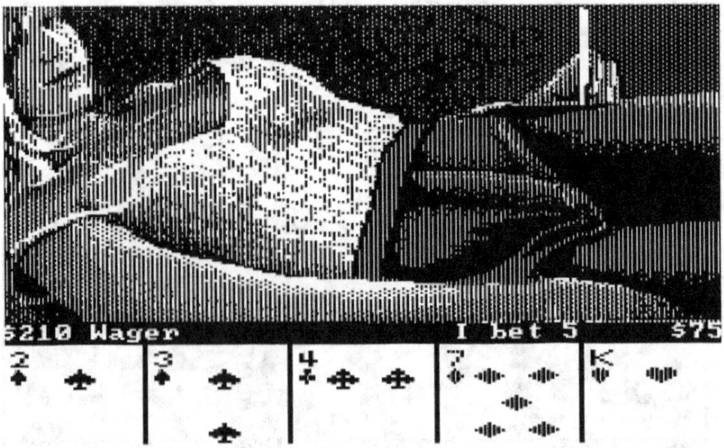

# The Fourth Ghost
# TRS-80

Creators: Don French and Steve Leininger
Company: Tandy, Radio Shack Production
Life: August 1977 - January 1981
Number of Sales: 215,000 (launch model)
Launch Cost: $599
Number of Games Titles: 1,361
Interpreter: TRSDOS
Microprocessor: Zilog Z80
Memory: 4K to 48K
Resolution: 64 x 16 characters
Colours: mono
Audio: via cassette port

So, ol' man Tandy comes out of Fort Worth in 1919 sellin' shoe leather, an' then Charlie Tandy Junior drifts from Texas Christian University straight into World War Two and out the other side again into the Tandy Corporation with a whole heap of stores doin' leatherwork and crafts and such. Then he gets his eye on a mail-order business called Radio Shack with a pat hand off a stacked deck, and sets out on the road to bein' a millionaire with his eighteen storey high Tandy Towers feedin' three thousand electronics stores by 1975. Oowee!

Well now, down there in among all the workin' men is a buyer dude name of Don French, and Don six months before gets hisself an assembly kit for a MITS Altair, who you will recall is the Number One Ghost in this here book. Don says to the boss he reckons their CB radio boom is gonna go bust, and they'll be hurtin' bad, but Tandy can make a killin' on the Next Big Thing if we can just come up with a ready-made version of this Altair machine. And the boss says there ain't nobody who knows spit about computers in Fort Worth, but they sure as hell got some nerds over in California. So that's where they heads on out to.

They find Steve Leininger workin' part-time in Paul Tyrell's store name of Byte Shop over in Mountain View, down the road apiece from National Semiconductor, and it so happens that Byte Shop is the first micro store in the US and they've just gotten delivery of Apple's first machine. Well, it also so happens that Steve's wife is hankerin' for him to quit for a better job, not to mention the pull of Texas not imposin' any state income tax. So they pack their bags faster than a sneeze through a screen door and Steve Leininger goes to work at Tandy with Don French in June 1976. Remember y'all the Commodore ain't gotten launched yet, and the Tandy brass want a kit like the Altair, exceptin' for savin' money for the bartender.

It's the hired nerd Steve Leininger who puts the spotlight on why the Altair is a pickle short of a barrel when he says there's just too many folk can't use a iron to solder with and what they all want is some device that's up and runnin' already like the Apple. So Don says to him okay, you go design one and I'll go sell it to our eleven million Tandy customers. Thing is, the average price of a Radio Shack item is thirty dollars, and you ain't gonna produce nothin' to whup an Altair for a lot less than ten times that.

Lieninger says they'll sell 50,000 machines codename TRS 80, standin' for Tandy Radio Shack (Zilog 80), and the Tandy brass says that's weapons-grade horseshit. But they go and agree to build 3,500 of me anyhow, 'cos that's one for each of their stores to do the accountin' on if nobody else out there gives a damn. They cut costs every which way, even savin' one-dollar-fifty a unit by cuttin' out the lower case characters in my display. In the end they spend a hundred and fifty thousand dollars to develop me before I hit the stores for $599 complete with my twelve-inch screen, real nice keyboard and cassette deck.

I make the pages of the press and they put it in print I can "do the payroll, teach children maths, store your favorite recipes, keep track of an investment portfolio, and play cards." Yowzah! It's those last two words that's the bell clapper. Fifteen thousand good folk jam the switchboard wantin' to buy me right there right then, and a quarter million more wants on the waitin' list for a hundred dollar deposit. I'm a machine that can play cards!

Thing is, Commodore and Apple got to rely on suppliers and assemblers and distributors and retailers and all, but at Tandy - well now, we got our own factories and we don't need nothin' from nobody else. Better still, we got our own shops all over the land. Anyways, in a couple of months all that waitin' list gets its ox out the ditch, and you can just walk in a Radio Shack store and walk out with me easy as eatin' striped candy. They sells 215,000 of my original, and by the time I gets retired all my versions tally 2,380,000 which you gotta admit is sweeter than stolen honey.

So that just about makes me the happiest ghost of all, and it's thanks to you gamers and the bald fact that there's more games written for me than all the other machines in creation until the Spectrum comes a long five years after my gravy train with biscuit wheels stops rollin'. Without li'l ol' me, thousands of games will never get wrote, and millions of gamers will never play 'em. Nearly alls my games gets designed by bedroom programmers, startin' out with type-ins from magazines like *Creative Computin'*, published by a guy with glasses and no necktie called Dave Ahl, a computer hacker from way back who cuts his teeth on a 1956 Burroughs. He goes bustin' the gates wide open with a book of 101 type-ins for me called *BASIC Computer Games*, and that little baby sells more than a million copies. You heard it right y'all, a million copies!

Know what I think, I think the Golden Age starts right there thanks to Dave. His book's got 'em all hogtied. There's strategy, arcade, simulation, puzzlers, action, adventure, table-top, sports, quiz-time, gamblin', everythin', all together. *Invaders, Breakout, MasterMind, Star Wars, Checkers, Poker, Rally, Lunar Lander, Roulette, Asteroids*, everythin' to keep a programmer's saddle oiled and a gamer's gun greased, all sewn up tight as a tick in them pages.

So why am I talkin' like this from beyond the grave? Well, it's not 'cause long as I got a biscuit, you got half, it's 'cause it's the way I always was. Anyways, I'm curious to knowin' how they gonna get the Fifth Ghost to talk to y'all? In Japanese? In Kraut? 'Cause next up, that old Sharp MZ-80 sure as hell don't come from Texas.

*above left: Charles Tandy, 1978* (with thanks to Elktracks Studio)
*above right: Steve Leininger, 1981* (with thanks to Hayden Publishing)
*below: David Ahl* (with thanks to The Dot Eaters)

*BASIC Computer Games, TRS-80 Edition, 1977*
*(with thanks to Centre For Computing History, NJ)*

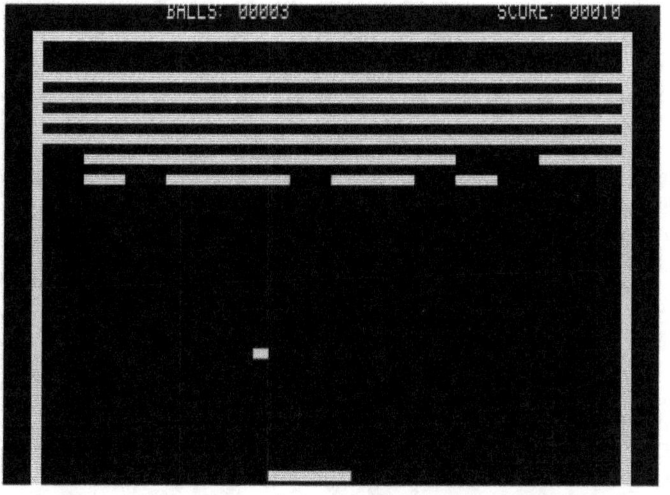


*above: Breakout for TRS80, 1978* *(with thanks to Elktracks Studio)*
*below: TRS Invaders, 1978* *(with thanks to The Dot Eaters)*

# The Fifth Ghost
# SHARP MZ-80

Creator: anonymous
Company: Sharp Corporation
Production Life: April 1978 to April 1981
Number of Sales: 97,000
Launch Cost: ¥85,000
Number of Games Titles: 76
Interpreter: BASIC
Microprocessor: Zilog Z80
Memory: 48K
Resolution: 40 x 25 characters, 320 x 200 pixels
Colours: mono
Audio: built-in speaker

In response to the previous ghost, of course I can communicate in English! And because I have been given this task then I will perform it faultlessly. I am the ghost of a Sharp MZ-80 home computer, and I will retain my dignity by not responding to any insults from other ghosts of their machines, such as the TRS-80 who was sired in a shack. Indeed, I will leave such things to the ghost that preceded me and the ghost that follows me, who both suffer from the misguided belief that Texas endows them with some sort of kudos. I can think of little to justify such kudos, apart, of course, from Beyoncé and Buddy Holly.

I was sired in Osaka, Japan, at the headquarters of the mighty Sharp Corporation, who at the time of my development were also creators of the world's first word processor, the first microwave oven, the first video cassette recorder, the first dual-cassette recorder, the first transistor calculator, and historically the creators of the first mechanical pencil which was called the Ever-Sharp, and is of course from whence my name was derived.

At the start of my commercial life in April 1978, I appeared in kit form in my native Japan only, but by 1979 I was marketed ready-made in Europe, finding particular favour with our historic wartime allies the Germans. As expected by both Japanese and German cultures, I was of utilitarian design, sturdily-constructed in my metal casing and of course extremely reliable, equipped to run a variety of high-level machine languages including Pascal, Fortran and the ubiquitous Basic.

It was not considered necessary to equip my launch model with high resolution or colour graphics, because my gamers were expected to be of a more cerebral nature. I was, however, equipped with a built-in speaker for gaming sound effects as well as a real-time clock to measure and monitor my gamers' performances.

My dedicated strategic role was to establish my manufacturer in the rapidly growing personal computer market and to allow a new generation of Japanese games designers to experiment hands-on for the first time. As such, my architecture was extremely clean, allowing my users to load software direct from my inbuilt cassette drive. Of course my keyboard was furnished with instant graphics and input for gaming symbols, as well as katakana characters in parallel with Western latinate characters.

An example of my use for the training of successful games designers was to be found with the brothers Yuji and Hiroshi Kudo, who went on to develop the globally successful *Bomberman*. They began their illustrious careers with me, by creating the excellent *Salad No Kuni Tomato*, in which Minister Pumpkin kidnaps Princess Tomato and brings terror to the vegetable kingdom. Naturally the player takes the heroic role of Sir Cucumber. Equally naturally, this graphics and text adventure is entirely conducted in Japanese although the program only understands commands for verbs and objects that are entered in English. A unique gaming strategy, you will admit.

One of my most popular games encouraged players to maintain punctuality within our highly efficient railway systems, and as such it was played against my highly accurate clock. It was called *Bōsō Orient Kyūkō*, and in it the gamer sped to the moving train by helicopter and got lowered to board it by rope, while avoiding common hazards like tunnels, mountains and ballistic missiles. Gameplay then moved on to having the player locate other passengers who might risk the integrity of the journey timetable, and killing them. Failure of the player to succeed or waste time in this mission resulted in them either going back a level or death, because our Japanese railways pride themselves on always sticking to their timetables.

A similar sense of civic duty and environmental awareness was engendered in another of my popular games, this one called *Walk Wan.* It was developed by the Tecno-Soft organisation, and I must assume that the anglicised misspelling was a deliberate marketing ploy. The title character of Wan was a large domestic dog and the gamer played the role of dog-walker. The action took place in an orderly small town set out on a grid system of pathways, where Wan and his canine relatives would deposit neat piles of coiled excrement hither and thither, in the road, by the picket fence and oftentimes conveniently at the open doorway of a dwelling. The player had to run around and collect all the faeces and then deposit them in the appropriate receptacle before Wan could create more. You cannot doubt why I am so proud to have brought such wholesome fun to the gaming world.

I hope this brief explanation of my role in the evolution of video gaming machines has been interesting and educational for you, and I regret that I do not have a larger allocation to explain to you why I should have conquered the world of micro computers in the Golden Age, but alas due to foreign interference and wanton imperialism I did not. And thus, before I say sayonara, a final word to the previous ghost, as typed in by one of my gamers and of which neither I nor the author have any control. ファッキュー、タンディ、何百万部も売れたかもしれないが、それでも君は無知な野郎だ。

*Personal Computer World cover, October 1979*
*(with thanks to Centre For Computing History, NJ)*

*above: MX-80K keyboard, 1978* (MC archive)
*below: Salad No Kuni Tomato, 1984* (with thanks to Yuji and Hiroshi Kudo)

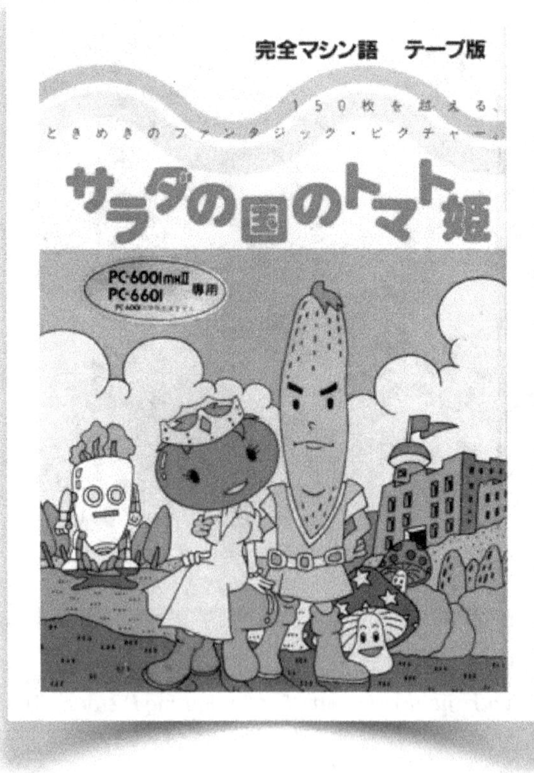

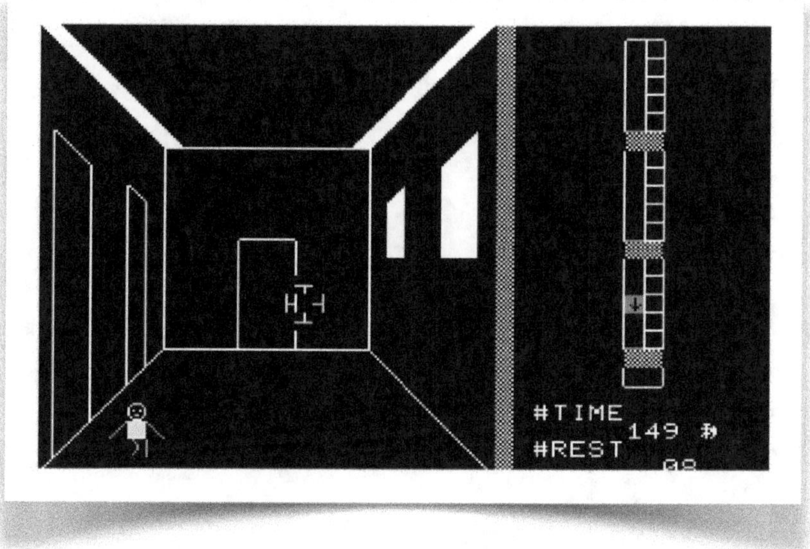


*above: Bōsō Orient Kyūkō, 1980 (with thanks to Toshiyuki Nagase)*
*below: Walk Wan, 1982 (with thanks to Tecno Soft)*

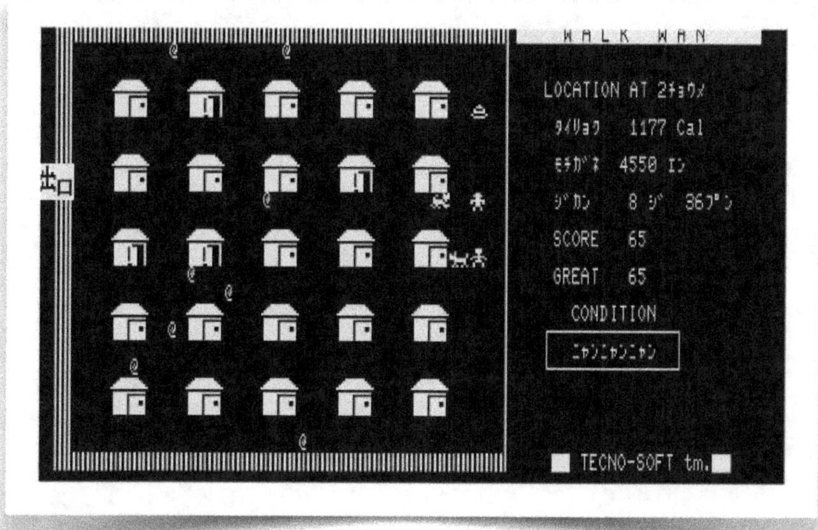

# The Sixth Ghost
# TI-99/4

Creator: Karl Guttag and unknown team
Company: Texas Instruments
Production Life: October 1979 to June 1981
Number of Sales: 18,600
Launch Cost: $1,150
Number of Games Titles: 55
Interpreter: TI BASIC
Microprocessor: TMS9900
Memory: 16K
Resolution: 252 x 196
Colours: 16
Audio: speaker, 3-channel

Here what I'm saying, there's lots of ghosts get triggered by PTSD, you know, but brother, I got it real bad. I got the flashbacks and the nightmares, and worst of all, man, I got the guilt. I just don't know what they was all thinking back then? I just don't know what they was expecting when they sent me out into battle alone? It wasn't my fault. They made me do stuff I just wasn't cut out to do. And I was only obeying orders, you know. They sent me out there from Fort Lubbock and then they went and abandoned me, and I can't forgive them for that. No sir, I just can't forgive them for that.

I was the first 16-bit home computer ever to get sent out there into battle, codename Mojo when I first got drafted. I gave you gamers the first sprites for your gaming, man, I even had a speech synthesiser, but my commanders messed up and forgot to prime it for me, then they just forced it as an add-on. And as well as software on cassette, my buddies knew I was different, man, because I could handle cartridges and floppy discs too. But when they sent me out against the Apple II my ass got whupped just about as bad as bad could be, you know. Brother, they never gave me the firepower, and I never had the back-up. I mean they just left me to die and then they junked me for the TI-99/4A which was more like a goddam console, man, a goddam console.

Yeah, sure, they had all their fancy battle plans where I was supposed to fit in the middle of a whole range of TI-99 machines, but none of them guys ever got released. Sure, I know I was more expensive than the Apple, and way way more than the PET, and I never even had a monitor, and my keyboard was so crappy it was only fit for a calculator, you know. And I know you know.

The commanders never had the mindset for a real fight, so all they thought to do was blame the government, I mean the Federal Communications Commission and their crazy rule that when I got connected to a TV set I couldn't cause no interference on the neighbour's receivers and such. They never did cure me of that, mind.

Man, I still get haunted by those first reports from the battlefield, like the one when the *New York Times* called me "an embarrassing failure." But what else could I have been, brother? The strategy guys at Texas Instruments thought I was some kind of appliance for morons, and they ignored gamers and creative folk who wanted to experiment and just have some home-grown fun. They never did develop a proper joystick for me, you know, and they never did bother with all that extra fuss to advertise me alongside their little calculators.

I'll tell you about my games, man, and it won't take me long. I reckon there was only fourteen games developed for me in my first year, and only another forty by the time I got abandoned, and even they was mostly just rip-offs and reruns from earlier titles for other machines. The only one I think was original was a strategy game called *Ant Wars*, and that went and got cloned a whole load of times for all the other machines that followed me. *Ant Wars* was a battle between a colony of red ants against a colony of black ants, and each ant gained a bit of strength or lost a bit of strength depending on what they did and what they ate, you know. I remember there was this spider and all, who didn't care what colour the ant was, it just went and ate them all up anyhow.

Another game I kinda liked was *Blackjack and Poker*, which had this great sound effect when I shuffled the cards, and some real groovy music for a winning hand. But even that game had a bug in it, because the gamer couldn't split the hand if I dealt a pair.

I had adventure games as well, and if I'd just had more time I could have given gamers some really great sounds and graphics to make them games a whole lot better, but I didn't have more time, I didn't, did I?

Let me think. Yes, I remember there was *Hunt the Wumpus* and that one started out as a text adventure for mainframes before I got a hold of it. It got played in this big old cave complex with bottomless pits and flying bats. It was really complicated with a top-down view of all the underground chambers and there was colour-coded clues, and trails of blood, and weird breezes drifting through, you know.

But the commanders didn't know diddly squat about games and gamers. There was too many chiefs and not enough indians, not enough indians for my games, man, I mean for my design. The commanders should never have gone for three different attacks all at the same time, I mean a low-end games console, a high-end business machine and me right there in the middle for hobbyists and such. Of course the squads went and started their own turf wars, and got fighting among themselves for resources and developers and such. And then that guy Peter van Cuylenburg the marketing commander went and commissioned some third-party contractor to design me. That's when I got codenamed Mojo.

But the hell with that, there's no point dwelling on what happened, it upsets me too much. In the end, the commanders had it coming, and they got what they deserved. They made a loss on home computers, must have been more than $250 million, and their stock value went and got wiped out, and Texas Instruments didn't just go lose the battle, they went and lost the whole friggin' war, man, the whole war. They just surrendered and quit the home computer battlefield altogether. They just walked a way, brother, they just walked away and left me here to die.

*above: TI-99/4 speech synthesiser insert, 1981* *(wih thanks to CFCH)*
*below: Blackjack & Poker, 1980* *(with thanks to Andy Frueh)*

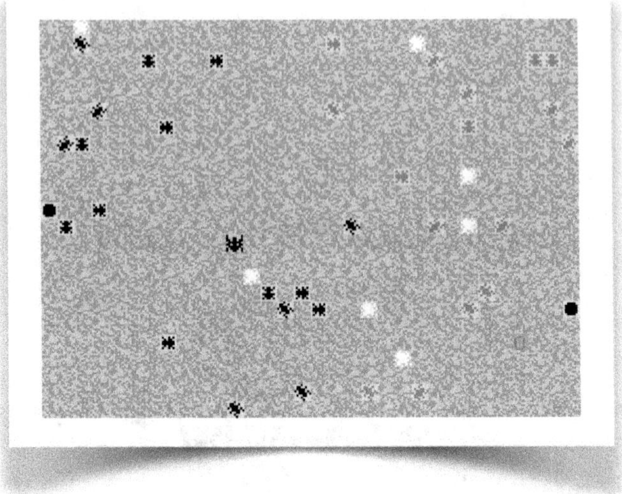

*above: Ant Wars, 1981* *(with thanks to Not-Polyoptics)*
*below: Hunt The Wumpus, 1980* *(with thanks to Kevin Kenney)*

# The Seventh Ghost
# ACORN ATOM

Creators: Herman Hauser, Chris Curry, Andy Hopper, Steve Furber, Sophie Wilson
Company: Acorn Computers
Production Life: March 1980 to January 1982
Number of Sales: 12,000
Launch Cost: £120 kit-form, £170 ready-made
Number of Games Titles: 36
Interpreter: Atom BASIC
Microprocessor: 6502
Memory: 2K
Resolution: 64 x 64 to 256 x 192
Colours: up to 4
Audio: speaker, single channel

I am the spirit of Acorn Atom, and I much prefer the term spirit for what I am, as opposed to ghost. I feel that a spirit has a much more positive association with machines that have been created to entertain, whereas a ghost merely implies a shadowy presence. And I don't feel ghostly either, I feel spiritual.

I hail from the university city of Cambridge, and I will not be the last spirit you meet from my illustrious city of learning and innovation. The reason for that is because of the huge influence on the history of microcomputers and the Golden Age of Gaming endowed by one man who was based here. Gamers of that era affectionately call him Uncle Clive, but seeing as I hardly knew him, I will refer to him by his formal title.

It was in 1977 that Sir Clive Marles Sinclair developed a cheap little computer kit he called the MK14, while working at his Science of Cambridge organisation alongside a physics postgraduate called Chris Curry. Instead of a keyboard for the input of commands, their little device boasted a rather primitive alpha-numeric keypad, but Sinclair was not very keen to add a properly functioning keyboard and then he lost interest in carrying the project any further. Curry, on the other hand, was very keen indeed to create a more user-friendly product based on microprocessors, and he persuaded a fellow alumnus from his year at Cambridge to join him, an Austrian fellow called Herman Hauser.

I promise that I will get to the point soon, but first I need to tell you that Curry and Hauser called their new company Cambridge Processor Unit because they thought it was a splendid conceit to exploit the abbreviation CPU. That was until they realised that what they really needed was a name to put them ahead of Apple Computers in the most accessible advertising medium of the day, the Yellow Pages of the telephone directory. For any young people reading this, a telephone directory was a large printed book containing the names, addresses and telephone numbers of subscribers, and the Yellow Pages were held in a section at the back of the book for businesses and services to advertise, so-called because it was printed on yellow paper. And so it was that they turned to the 14th century proverb 'mighty oaks from little acorns grow,' and registered the brand name Acorn Computers. Personally, I would have made doubly sure of all things alphabetical in those Yellow Pages by exploiting the name Aardvark, but that has since been grabbed by a landmine clearance company.

To continue, off they went to scout for the brightest students at the university, where they came across Steve Furber who was already building computers for fun, and Roger Wilson who had already designed the single-board micro that would become my heart and soul, first as the Acorn System 1, then the Acorn System 2 and finally as my beautiful complete package which they now called their Acorn Atom. You will hear more about Roger Wilson when you get to the Tenth Ghost in this book, by which time she will be Sophie Wilson, on her way to becoming Commander of the Order of the British Empire and among the Top Ten most important women in the entire history of technology. But please stick with me here if you can resist the temptation to skip ahead.

And so it was that I became a perfect example of nominative determinism, the Acorn Atom. Acorn, which represents the origin of the oak trees that built the ships of the British navy on which a global empire was founded. And Atom, which not only echoed the atomic age in which we all exist but also represented the fundamental building blocks of all things, and with which another global empire was about to be born; the creative empire of gaming. The author of my user manual was David Johnson-Davies, a Cambridge experimental psychologist who founded Acornsoft, and he had the wit to title my user-manual *Atomic Theory and Practice*.

When I became available for the new empire builders to experiment with, distinct genres of video games had coalesced, and each one of of them combined only three basic elements: hand-eye coordination, logical deduction and randomised chance. When I was designed, transliterations of universal board games and gambling games were available for every home computer on the planet. Adaptations of arcade games and traditional sports themes like ping-pong had been among the first video games of all, and mazes and platform games were similarly easy to adapt. First-person and third-person shooters had begun to appear in the form of rudimentary blobs and crude shapes moving around the screen, with basic scene-setting achieved by a few words of text for themes like sci-fi, westerns, military, fantasy, heroes and the like. A sub-genre of these was also beginning to appear in the form of beat 'em-ups, stealth and survival games, with primitive action adventures also written to fit within the limitations of our limited memories.

There were only three official games released for me in the year of my launch 1980, *3d Noughts and Crosses*, which was not in 3D at all, a terrible version of *Othello*, and a supposed adventure game called *Demon Dungeon* which had no demons or dungeons and was mostly a grid of numbers. Not an auspicious start, I admit.

To be truthful there were only 36 games titles released for me during my entire production run, which is similarly unimpressive, however ten of those titles were compilations. In 1981 Acornsoft released nine compilation packs, imaginatively titled *Gamespack 1* through to *Gamespack 9*, with three games in each pack. And then in an act of bravado, at the start of 1982 *Gamespack 10* appeared which included ten games to round things off. My actual tally of individual games was 72.

But that wasn't the point. The previous spirits and

ghosts in their machines mostly fluttered outside of the UK, and particularly in the USA gamers were more interested in ready-mades and type-ins rather than programming their own entertainments. Over here in the United Kingdom it was somewhat different, and I was the first home-grown machine where British talent could get to grips creating games software for themselves. And although I only sold 12,000 units, those units were the springboard for what was to follow. And what was to follow was a revolution that allowed the UK to become the hub of excellence in games creation for the next ten years.

There were in fact hundreds of games written for me by my users, possibly thousands, and it goes without saying that almost all of them were derivative rubbish. Clones of clones. But they were our derivative rubbish, and our training ground for enthusiasts and amateurs and wide-eyed youngsters. My personal favourite of the derivative rubbish written for me was *Bouncing Babies*, an unashamed rip-off of the Japanese Game & Watch handheld game *Fire!* The player had to rescue babies falling from a burning high-rise, by bouncing them on a trampoline before they got splattered. And that, my friends, is the perfect metaphor for the entire future gaming industry, as will be revealed in this very book. I was soon swept away by something that unleashed the start of a global industry from bedrooms to billions. Read on, my friends, read on, and know that my spirit remains undimmed.

*above left: Chris Curry, 1982* (with thanks to Centre for Computing History)
*above right: Herman Hauser, 1990* (with thanks to Centre for Computing History)
*below left: Roger Wilson, 1983* (with thanks to Redwood Publishing)
*below right: Steve Furber, 1983* (with thanks to Redwood Publishing)

*Atomic Theory and Practice*, 1980 (David Johnson-Davies)

*above: Bug-Byte software advert, 1982* (with thanks to Centre for Computing History)
*below: Bouncing Babies, 1981* (with thanks to Dave Baskin)

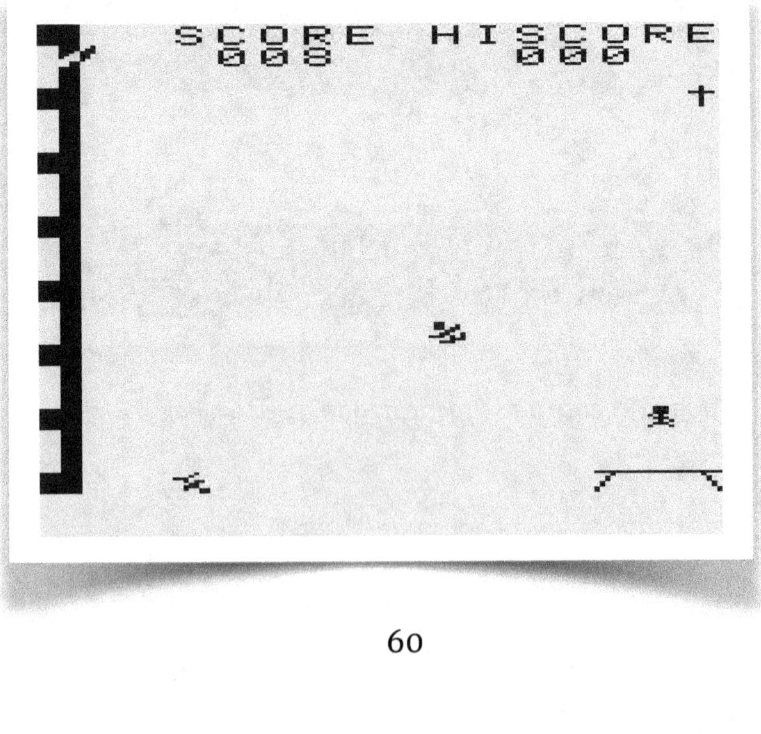

# The Eighth Ghost
# VIC 20

Creator: Michael Tomczyk
Company: Commodore Business Machines
Production Life: September 1980 to January 1985
Number of Sales: 2,500,000
Launch Cost: $299.95
Number of Games Titles: 953
Interpreter: Commodore BASIC
Microprocessor: MOS 6502
RAM Memory: 5K
Resolution: 176 x 184
Colours: 16
Audio: 4-voice

Did you ever read crap like that asshole Acorn Atom spirit wrote? What a truckload of baloney about Great Britain as the birthplace of the gaming revolution. I mean is that meant to be a joke or what? Gimme a break and go take a hike, buster, you had zilch games and you had zilch sales. You wanna know who started the gaming revolution? Well look no further because here I am, the Commodore VIC-20, the first home computer to sell a million and the longest run of any machine in this here entire book. Go suck on your Univershitty of Cambilge, because Daddy's here. And speaking of daddies, mine was Jack Tramiel. Big Daddy himself!

Back in April 1980, President Jack made Michael S. Tomczyk Vice-President at Commodore. And he gave him the codename Godfather, and after Tomczyk designed me Jack gave him the codename The Czar, that's right, The Czar. So go screw Ginger Sinclair because it was Tomczyk who changed the gaming world. It was Tomczyk who made me, and he was a goddam US Army hero, Commendation Medal Korea, Bronze Star Vietnam and a personal friend of Starfleet Captain James T. Kirk, not some bald-head, google-eye loser from Middle-sex, London, England.

OK. Before you go asking, there's no real reason I got called VIC-20, no reason. The advertising always called me the Friendly Computer, real friendly, and Vic was just a real friendly type name, the kind of friendly type name for a bar-tender or maybe a barber, and Vic was short for Victory too. And the same goes for the 20, it meant nothing, nada. It just sounded good when you spoke it, you know. VIC-20, Vic Twenty, like a call sign from a truck driver best buddy.

My BASIC commands were just about the same as my heavy-metal brother the Commodore PET, and President Jack and Veep Tomczyk targeted me at what they called "the cottage industry developers", the bedroom boys, the garage gang, and they went right out there to capture new games-maker recruits. That's what they did. Not like those idiots at Texas Instruments who tried to ban homegrown software and favor their own titles. I was pushed out to gamers right from the start. Gamers, gamers, gamers. And that's why Tomczyk drafted in the main man, top gun Scott Adams, the founder of Adventure International.

Scott was the first guy to write adventure style games for personal computers, and he'd already had hits with material for the TRS-80 and the Apple II, so my boss made him a deal to rewrite his five top seller adventures for me straight off. Top five. Trouble was, they took up 16K of RAM memory a piece, and I only had 5K, but no problem. The neat trick was to sell the games as plug-in cartridges instead of having them load in on cassette tape like on the rival machines. Well, I can tell you guys, our first production run of those adventure cartridges hauled in over a million and a half dollars, and Vic-20 was on the path to victory. VICtory. And that wasn't all, Tomczyk didn't just design me on my own, he was so way ahead of his time he went and designed me a modem. Can you believe that, my own modem. First modem at under a hundred dollars, first one, very first. And they went and sold a million of my modems. More than a million.

So, back to Scott Adams. I'm telling you, Scott was the first celebrity games author, and I'm not too proud to say I owe him one hell of a lot for helping me win my battle to dominate the world of gaming. In fact he helped me so much I'm gonna list all his adventure titles for me right here right now. Ready? Here we go. *Adventureland, Pirate Adventure, Mission Impossible, Voodoo Castle, The Count, Strange Odyssey, Mystery Fun House, Pyramid of Doom, Ghost Town, Savage Island* and *Golden Voyage*. And if you go look at their cover-art at the end of this chapter, you'll see it was just about as crappy as crappy can be, but my gamers loved it all the same. They loved it. Loved it.

On the other hand, my own screen graphics were pretty darn good. In fact they were great. My default was 176 by 184 pixels, sixteen colours and any colour border all round the screen. Like my older brother PET, I had two different sets of 256 characters each and I had reverse video for every one of them in both sets. I could handle 4x8 lo-res characters with three colours in each, and I had a hi-res mode for each character in 8x8 single colour. Sure, that looked a bit blocky, a bit blocky, but hell we're talking 1980 and we're talking less than three hundred bucks. Besides, my audio was the best you could get, with triple generators for three-octave pulse waves and another white-noise generator for special effects, and I had a volume control on each one. Each one. All four. And if my games designers hit the right buttons, I could hit a five-octave range. That limey Acorn Atom didn't even come close, not for graphics and not for sound. Not even close.

I've told you I could handle cartridges for games and extra memory, and I was ready to roll with our Datassette cassette drive, and my VIC-1540 disk drive, and Atari joysticks, and a load of printers and of course the other revolution that was only just starting - like I already told you, my very own personal modem!

Seeing as I'm the ghost in every single one of my two and a half million machines, just don't expect me to reckon up how many home-made games got created on me altogether. But there was near on a thousand commercial games published, and it was me who made sure the Golden Age of video games went mainstream right there in the homes all over America. All over the world. Whole world. My biggest titles were all classics, and they had the biggest names behind them too. That's right, the biggest.

Sega ported their *Star Trek* for me, including a real cheesy version of the TV theme tune, Broderbund licensed

*Choplifter* in a great version, Atarisoft gave me their own conversion of Nintendo's *Donkey Kong*, Parker Brothers licensed me Konami's *Tutankham* and I know my *Jelly Monsters* was one of a whole load of *PacMan* clones, but it sure was the best. And it was the best by a hell of a long way. The same goes for my *Vic Avenger*, the best ever version of *Space Invaders*. And they say my *Gorf* was the greatest arcade game for any home micro of the time, for the gameplay, and the graphics and the audio too. For everything.

The great thing about being a ghost is I can listen in on what gamers are saying and thinking not just from here and now, but from back in the day. And when I read the minds of old-timer Gamers for their all-time favourites, they all say the winner is my classic shoot-em-up called *Omega Race*, the only arcade game Bally Midway ever did with vector graphics. It was written by Ron Halliburton, who cut his teeth at Allied Leisure in the 1960s and looked just like Colonel Sanders. Thanks Ron, you gave me my top-seller and folks are still playing that one to this day.

Well folks, you can skip the next two chapters about snot-nose limey stuff and get to the next real machine in the Commodore story, all about my kid brother the Commodore 64. I mean, what is it with you Brits thinking you can compete with the US of A when it comes to computers and games. Will you answer me that, huh? Don't bother. I'll sue you anyway.

*above: VIC-20 box lid, 1980* *(with thanks to the Strong National Museum of Play)*
*below: VIC Modem, 1980* *(with thanks to the Strong National Museum of Play)*

*above: Scott Adams 12 adventure titles, 1981* (*with thanks to The Dot Eaters*)
*below: Omega Race score chart, 1981* (*MC archive*)

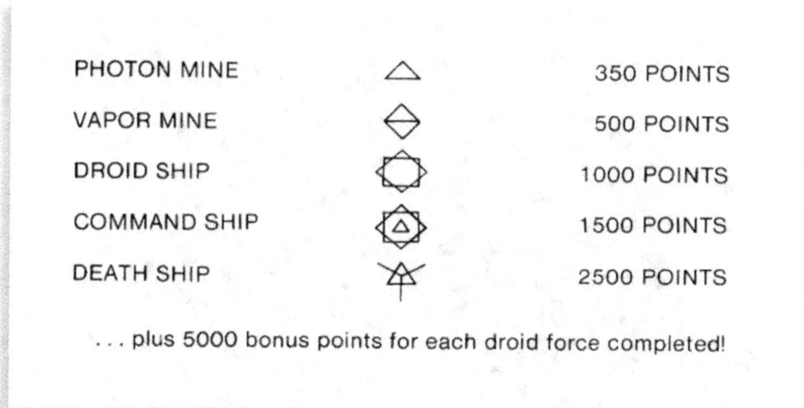

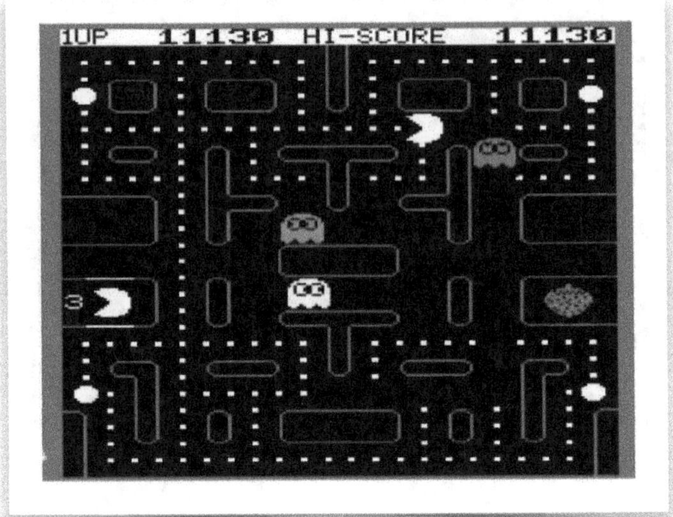


*above: Jelly Monsters, 1981* *(with thanks to HAL Laboratory)*
*below: Gorf, 1981* *(with thanks to David Nutting)*

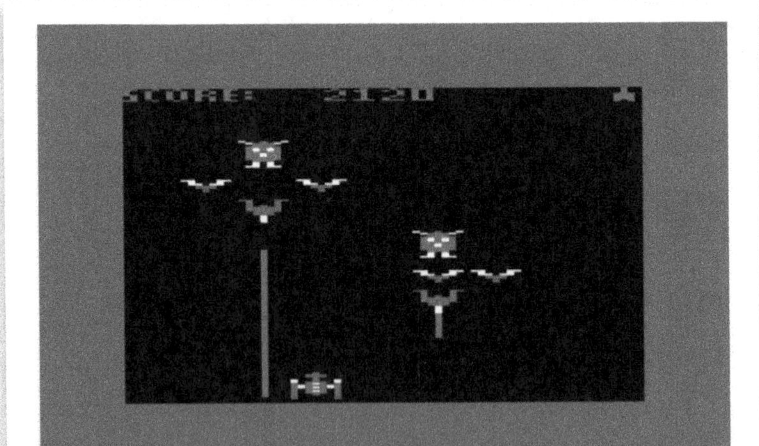

# The Ninth Ghost
# ZX81

Creator: Rick Dickinson
Company: Sinclair Research
Production Life: March 1981 to April 1984
Number of Sales: 1,512,000
Launch Cost: £49.95 (kit), £69.95 (assembled)
Number of Games Titles: 305
Interpreter: Sinclair BASIC
Microprocessor: Z80
Memory: 1KB
Resolution: 64x48 pixels, 24 lines x 32 characters
Colours: monochrome
Audio: none

I'm black and I'm proud. I'm Scottish and I'm skittish, ye ken. I'm the greatest little thing to come out of Dundee since *The Beano*. Ah, I remember the old Timex factory of Dundee with fondness. It had fallen on such hard times after the traditional business of watch-making collapsed, and it had left our highly skilled workforce high and dry with sod all to do. I'm not sure if Timex was chosen to make me because of altruism or cynical exploitation, but it was a happy day when my contract got signed.

I'm less than seven inches square, about the size and weight of a cheese toastie, and I'm a tenth the cost of dear auld Altair who kicked off this book, with four times the memory and sixty times the sales. Not bad going in less than seven years since the start of the Golden Age. Not bad at all.

Aye, I know I'm black, but like all good Scots my roots are ginger and beardy, with both Clive Sinclair who funded me and Rick Dickinson who designed me. And if you want to know more about them there's enough to fill a library out there, I'm going to stick to the inside story of my part in the gaming bonanza. It was Bill Clinton or some other numpty who said, "keep it simple, stupid", so let's begin with how ridiculously simple I am.

I plug straight in to a home TV set nae bother. I've got no moving parts, not even an on/off switch. I've got no keyboard, just a layer of plastic to trigger my pressure-sensitive layout of numbers, letters, graphics, controls and commands. Dickinson was dead canny, I won more design awards than any home micro before me. And it was because I was so simple that I became part of the lives of the general public and not just for hobbyists and business. I became part of their lives not because of anything technical or clever, it was because it was so simple to create games with me. Aye it was. Hundreds of folk started to produce their own entertainment with me, then thousands. And thousands of folk started playing games on me, then hundreds of thousands.

Let me tell you that it was in the year of Our Lord 1792 that William Henry Smith inherited his father's newspaper shop. By the time I came along, WH Smith had 1,700 stores in over thirty countries, and let us bless them for the decision to sell me to the masses. I was the first low-cost machine available over the counter in almost every High Street in the land, and where WH Smith led, the other chain stores followed. When I arrived all across the UK in 1981, home computing was a niche pastime. By the time I left in 1984 it was a major industry. When I started, gamers would gather together in small groups to share and enjoy their hobby. When I left, tens of thousands of enthusiasts were flocking to games shows at the biggest arenas in the land, and my ZX Microfairs had become a big auld joyful institution.

Gamers today can have no idea how inventive and creative programmers had to be in my day. Remember, they only had 1KB of memory to exploit for absolutely everything, all the routines, all the commands, all the graphics, all the animations, everything in one wee kilobyte. Today's average game eats up around 150,000,000 times as much - per hour! Even with a notoriously wobbly RAM pack up my behouchie the maximum they had was 16K, and the extra charge for that was as much as I cost in the first place. But I'm not complaining.

Now I'd like to keek at some of the games those pioneers managed to stuff inside my memory and tell you why they were so good. In April 1981 Linda Evans bought her hubby Malcolm a ZX81 for his thirty-seventh birthday and also because he needed cheering up after his workplace shut down. He'd taken up playing the classical guitar and lute, and it was at a guitar session that he met JK Greye who had some good ideas for a video game and set up a software company to produce it. Malcolm got programming and by November he came up with the all-time classic *3D Monster Maze*, and when I say classic, I mean classic. He only had my low-res block graphics, but he pioneered four braw things. Thing One, the survival horror game. Thing Two, the 3D random maze generator. Thing Three, the first-person viewpoint. Thing Four, emotional interaction between the monster and the player. His legacy still lives on in thousands of 3D survival games, except they take up a hundred million times more memory than I could give him.

About the same time as I arrived on the scene, a schoolteacher called Don Priestley took his son along to enrol for a night-school computing course, and Don decided to join the course as well. His son dropped out, but Don kept it up, and in 1982 he wrote one of my all-time favourites. It was called *Mazogs*, and it was a cross between a maze game and an adventure quest with its own instruction booklet. Well, not so much a booklet as a folded sheet of paper, but a whole lot better than most. There were three properly different levels, and the way he created real atmospherics from my block graphics was a miracle. I have tried to forgive him for going on to write *Benny Hill's Madcap Chase*, but baws to it I can't. After inflicting that horror on the gaming community he had the grace to quit and go back to teaching.

My audacity prize for squeezing the last pixel of graphics has to go to Jim Bagley for his *Dragon's Lair*, the biggest game ever ported for me. Thanks Jim, and I still say you were in *The Mother's of Invention*. As for orthodox ports, let's hear it for the disciple of Sandy White's *Ant Attack*. It wasn't pretty, but it was genuine 3D isometrics.

No time for false modesty as I tell you I became the top-selling computer in the UK by a Scottish mile, and then set my eyes on the world market, particularly America. A bit like when The Beatles re-exported rock'n'roll back to America, I used my connections with Timex to do the same for home computers. At first Timex sold me in to the USA as the ZX-81, but the factory just couldn't keep pace with demand so Timex Portugal took on the business of manufacture and export for the American market, where I was known as the Timex Sinclair and T/S 1000. I can verify 400,000 US sales in my first year there, and another 100,000 in Canada, but this is where my stats go a bit haywire. Timex Portugal kept making me years after the Dundee factory stopped, and they claimed 800,000 sales in Poland alone. Personally, I doubt that very much, but hey, I was already ghostly by then.

There were some pretty good semi-legal clones, with names like Marathon, Tonel, Futura and Polybrain, and like most of your other ghosts in the machine, a whole bunch of illegal clones and unauthorised fakes arrived on the scene, all claiming to be me. Brazil was top of the illegal league table, with Argentina on silver and South Korea on bronze. And if imitation is the sincerest form of flattery, then I am greatly flattered.

Before I hand you over to that usurper, the treacherous BBC Micro, let me leave you with a misquotation written in 1875, from *Holy Willie's Prayer* by Robert Burns, my nation's greatest poet.

*All in this spotty, misty clime,*
*I backward mused on wasted time,*
*How I had spent my youthful prime*
*An' done nae-thing,*
*But stringing nonsense up to rhyme*
*For fools to sing.*

Thank you for reading this. Haste ye back.

*above: Rick Dickinson, 1981* (with thanks to Retro Gamer)
*below: ZX81 wobbly RAMpack, 1981* (MC archive)

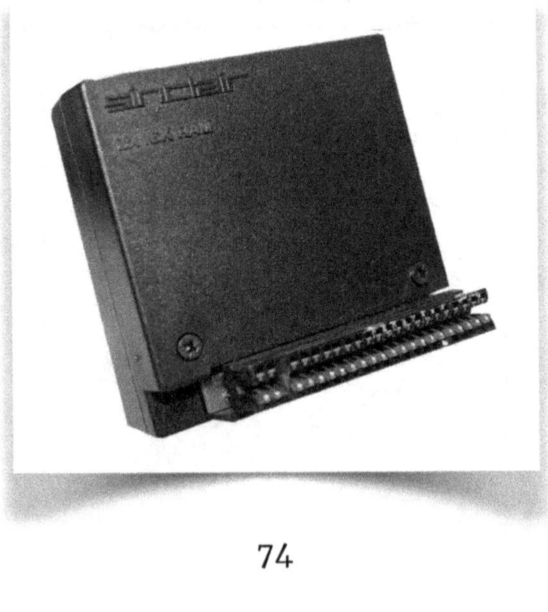

*above: 3D Monster Maze, 1981* (with thanks to Malcolm Evans)
*below: Malcolm Evans, 1982* (with thanks to Rachel Evans)

*above: Dragon's Lair, 1983 (with thanks to Jim Bagley)*
*below: Jim Bagley, 2022 (with thanks to Planeta Sinclair)*

*above: Don Priestley* (with thanks to Retronauts)
*below: Mazogs* (with thanks to Don Priestley)

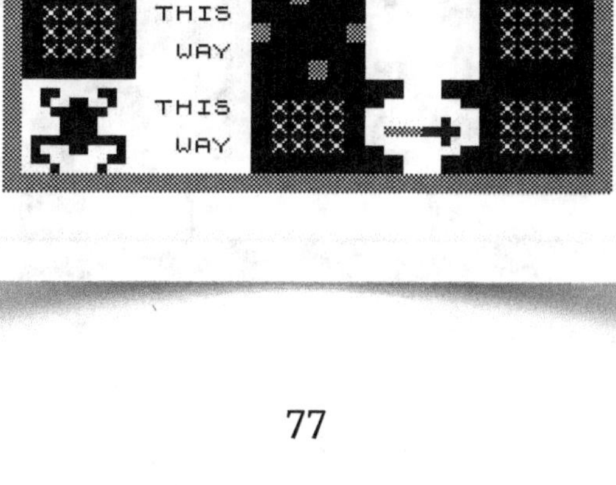

*above: Sandy White* (*with thanks to Sinclair User*)
*below: Ant Attack* (*with thanks to Sandy White*)

# The Tenth Ghost
# BBC MICRO

Creators: Sophie Wilson and Steve Furber
Company: Acorn Computers
Production Life: December 1981 to July 1985 (Model A)
Number of Sales: 1,600,000
Launch Cost: £235
Number of Games Titles: 1,370
Interpreter: Acorn MOS
Microprocessor: MOS 6502
Memory: 16/32K
Resolution: 640x256
Colours: 8
Audio: 4 channel mono

I have a question for you. Why are most of the other ghosts in these machines concerned with dry technical details and dusty personal anecdotes, or with scurrilous business shenanigans and backstabbing? Surely what you want are inside stories about your favourite games so you can wallow in nostalgia and relive the heady excitement of the times. In which case I intend to go straight to the heart of the matter and tell you about the most pivotal and important games that were created for my players to enjoy. Perhaps after that, if I have the time and inclination, I'll dish the dirt on anyone and everyone who has it coming. Do we have a deal? Excellent. Then let me begin.

My favourite games have all got one thing in common and that is the fact they were written by teenagers. My all-time top BBC Micro game has got to be *Elite*, and that's an opinion shared by most of my gamers too. It was so much more than a space-trading extravaganza. For starters it was non-linear, it was also open ended, it was a pioneer of wire-frame 3D, it monitored your response time and it tweaked the action accordingly, and to cap it all it came complete with a science fantasy novella by Bob Holdstock. And that book was an award-winner too, like the game itself which was created by Ian Bell and Dave Braben, a pair of high-flyer teenagers from the central casting emporium of Jesus College. Thanks boys.

My next best favourite is the one called *Chuckie Egg*, by sixteen year-old bedroom gamer Nigel Alderton, and I'm not too proud to admit that he originally wrote it for the Speccy. Probably the best platform and ladders game of its day. It took him five months to write, which was a long, long time back then, when many young writers were knocking out inferior efforts for me in weeks if not days.

Who's next? Ah yes, I'd like to give a shout out to Nick Pelling for my scrolling platformer *Frak!* with just about the best cartoon graphics ever for me, and it had fabulous use of my colour palette too. Nick was a late-teenager when he wrote this classic, then he got a bit sidetracked and didn't complete his MBA until thirty years later. But he did get a distinction, which is nice.

Let's have another one. Michael Jakobsen was still at college in Denmark when he knocked out *Citadel*, a game that I put right up near the top of my innovations chart. He allowed the gamer to choose the sex of their on-screen character, and unlike most other designers he didn't kill you off with enemies and hazards, but instead you got maimed a trifle and then lost energy during conflict. He also introduced some rather realistic sound effects and a cool synthetic speech intro. Excellent.

Simon Pick was even younger than the rest. He started programming at school when he was still only fourteen and his first commercial game was *Dare Devil Denis*. It was totally based on Atari's *Stunt Cycle* from 1977, but this was Thatcher's Britain, and she would have applauded blatant rip-offs, opportunism and youthful enterprise like his. And so we come to the sordid business of my own opportunism and rise to power, which I will reveal for you as honestly as I can.

The venerable British Broadcasting Corporation had been banging on about the impact of computers for several years to anyone who would listen or watch, and in 1981 they commissioned a new educational series. Importantly, they managed to get the British government to back the series via a national Computer Literacy Project. It was just about the most ambitious scheme that had ever been proposed up to then, it helped make Britain the most computer literate country on the planet and it inspired a generation of coders and gamers. Don't tell me that this was achieved by Clive Sinclair, it wasn't.

What the BBC wanted more than anything was their

very own micro to go with the campaign. So they invited seven UK manufacturers to bid for the job including Sinclair, but he'd just launched his ZX81 and his eye was off the ball long enough for Chris Curry here at Acorn Computers to doorstep the BBC and invite them to come and view the perfect machine, which he claimed was sitting in Acorn headquarters in Cambridge. The first problem was that he was so persuasive and the BBC were so keen they said they would view it the following week on the same day they were due at Sinclair Research. The second problem was that Acorn's perfect machine didn't actually exist. So Chris asked his partner Herman Hauser to lie to our designers Sophie Wilson and Steve Furber and tell each of them that the other had agreed to have my prototype ready by Friday. That was on the Monday.

It was a deception that paid off big time. My circuit board and innards were designed by Wednesday night, I was assembled on Thursday and my operating system was ported over on Friday morning. When the BBC assessors arrived on Friday afternoon they were greeted by me merrily rendering a simple pattern on a hi-res screen. After a four hour break, while the assessors popped along the road to see what Sinclair had to offer, I was able to show them full text and graphics, and so it was that I won the beauty contest.

The Oric and Dragon were also contenders, but I'll let them tell you their stories in their own chapters. Everybody knows that it was Clive Sinclair who threw a hissy fit and immediately set about producing a cheapo rival to me which became the Spectrum. Well yah-boo sucks to him. The Speccy was way less sophisticated than me, but because it was so cheap it did really well in the home market.

Meanwhile I was guaranteed gold-plated success because I monopolised the schools market as well as the BBC airwaves. So much so, that within two years Acorn floated on the London Stock Exchange for over a hundred million pounds. Sorry Clive. Well no, I'm not really sorry at all, in fact I had to laugh when he told *Practical Computing* magazine,

"By God the BBC should not be making computers any more than they should be making BBC cars or BBC toothpaste."

Not content with monopolising the UK Schools market, Acorn tried to pull the same stunt for me in the USA. There were reports that US schools placed orders worth over twenty million dollars via a network of a thousand dealers, but I'm very sad to tell you that this was hopelessly optimistic. In fact it was what a cynic might call a bare-faced lie.

I had a little more luck in India, where the government emulated the UK and started its own computer literacy program, adopting me wholesale along with my educational software. But the clone wallahs soon moved in with boringly named copies like SCL and less boring names like Dolphin. But it was all education, education, education, and their gamers were never really catered for. In fact no original games of real merit emerged from the enterprise at all.

But the Golden Age was good to me, and thanks to the BBC I had a superb long run. And it was thanks to their efforts in educating a generation of schoolchildren and students that I had masses of games written for me in my native land. My choice of favourites may not be your choice, but I am in command of my own destiny, and allowed to tell you what I like. And that my dear reader is no lie.

*above: BBC Computer Literary Project launch, 1982* (with thanks to BBC Rewind)
*below: Elite, 1984* (with thanks to David Braben & Ian Bell)

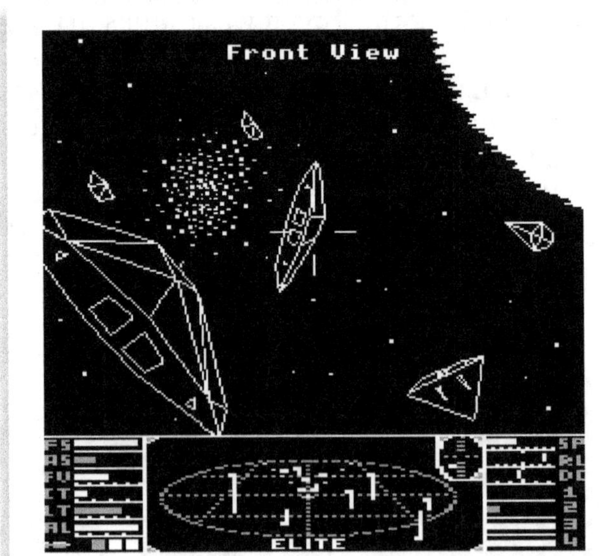

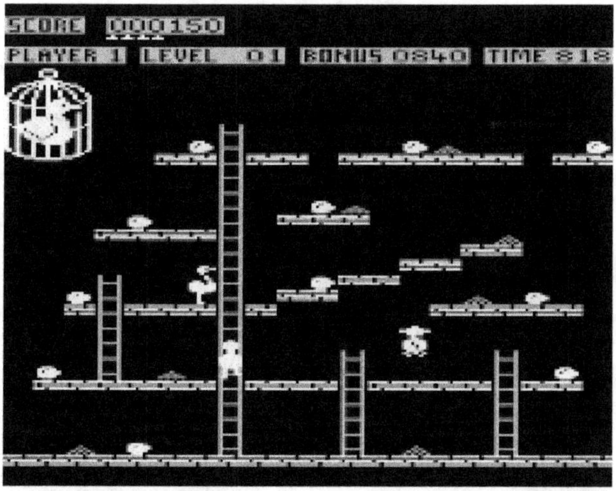


*above: Chuckie Egg, 1983* *(with thanks to Nigel Alderton)*
*below: Frak! 1984* *(with thanks to Nick Pelling)*

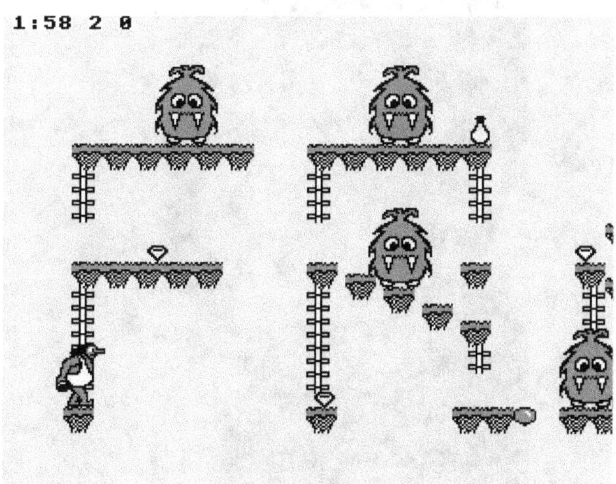

*above: Citadel, 1985* *(with thanks to Michael Jakobsen)*
*below: Simon Pick, 1985* *(with thanks to Simon Pick)*

# The Eleventh Ghost
# COMMODORE 64

Creator: Al Charpentier
Company: Commodore Business Machines
Production Life: August 1982 - April 1994
Number of Sales: 12,594,000
Launch Cost: $595 / £399
Number of Games Titles: 5,686
Interpreter: Commodore BASIC
Microprocessor: MOS 6510/8500
Memory: 64K
Resolution: 320 x 200
Colours: 16
Audio: dedicated SID chip, 3 voices

Hi there fans! It's me, the one you've been waiting for. I'm the Ghost of the C64, the top-seller micro in history. If you go tote up all the sales of all the other machines in this book, then my lifetime sales beat all of them put together. And I'll let you in on a little secret... just like that BBC Micro in the last chapter, I was put together in days. Not months, not weeks, but days.

There was this real nice guy called Al Charpentier, and he had designed the chips for my older brother VIC-20. He said to me, "I was fresh out of ideas for whatever chips the rest of the world wanted, so I decided to produce state-of-the-art video and sound chips for the world's best video games machine." Well, our Commodore Big Boss Jack Tramiel said that was fine and dandy, but if I was set to replace my older brother VIC then I had to be real easy to use and real cheap to buy. And one more thing, I had to have more memory than any of my competitors. A whole lot more memory.

My body was just a hand-me-down from brother VIC and my circuit board was the same size too, so the only thing the marketing boys did was change the colour of my plastic casing and stick on a new label. It was Al's chip that made me a winner.

Mind you, it wasn't all plain sailing, because Al went and quit soon after I got launched, and a rumour went round that he'd gone and left me with a bug in my video chip that caused a weird snowstorm effect on screen. But that was nothing but a dirty lie. The real problem was in my ROM chip, but it only affected a few machines and it got cured in a couple of weeks. The thing is, after Christmas 1982 one hell of a price-war broke out in the games micro market, and The Boss ordered my price to be slashed by two hundred bucks. So what happened was a whole load of gamers who had got me for Christmas went and claimed I was faulty with the snowstorm bug, when all the while there was absolutely nothing wrong with me, and they got their full-price money back while I was still under my 90-day warranty. Then they just went and bought me again for the new lower price. Ha, ha! I don't blame them one bit, and in fact it gave me a few valuable weeks to get my ducks in a row.

If I was going to be The World's Best Video Games Machine then what I needed was The World's Best Video Game as an exclusive, and thanks to a mystery twenty-three year-old Brit called Andrew Spencer, that's exactly what I got. His *International Soccer* was a classic from the get-go and it set the benchmark for competitive sport games from the day it got launched. The pace was real fast, the competition gameplay was great, and players felt like they were right there in the middle of the action. As soon a group of friends got playing, everyone wanted to buy a copy for themselves, and I was the only machine they could play it on. I lost count of the number of times that game topped the charts, and all the while my sales were racking up.

In fact they racked up so fast that as soon as the *Ghostbusters* movie came out, its franchise game got licensed for me first. OK, so it ain't necessarily a classic, but it boosted my sales even more, along with another spin-off movie game that really was a classic, and that one was *Bruce Lee*. It was a beat-em-up monster mixed up with a platform game, and most of all it was fun! When it topped the charts all over the world it helped prove I was here to stay, and it helped prove I could handle all sorts of games in all sorts of styles.

*Pitstop II* was a great one for me too, and it gave my gamers the feel of a real arcade game they could play at home. The 3D track was from the racing driver's view, but you could also have it split-screen, so first it encouraged my gamers to play against one another and just like with *International Soccer* they soon got the notion to go get me for themselves.

I wasn't just the best seller of any home computer ever, I was the longest in production too. Fourteen years, no messing. So I'll move you on and tell you what I think are the three best games that came out in what I reckon was the Golden Year of the Golden Age. Ronald Reagan was in the White House, Mike Tyson was world boxing champ, and Michael Jackson tried to buy the corpse of The Elephant Man. The year was 1987 and the three games were *Wizball*, from Sensible Software in the UK, *Bubble Bobble* from Taito over there in Japan, and *The Great Giana Sisters* from Rainbow Arts in Germany. Let's hear it for *Wizball* first.

John Hare and Chris Yates knew each other from school, and when they got to growing hair and beards and stuff, they set up Sensible Software and won themselves no less than seven Number One hit games. *Wizball* was voted Game Of The Decade, and I'm not going to argue with that. I guess you'd call it a psychedelic shooter game, and the movement really was something else. Everything obeyed the laws of physics until it didn't, and once you got used to handling those controls it had real depth to it, plus great graphics and some neat jokes. But if Sensible Software was new to the gaming world, Taito was an old hand.

Taito is still based in Tokyo, where they started out in the early 1950s making jukeboxes from busted machines on US military bases. But it was video gaming where they made history when they gave us the original *Space Invaders* in 1978. When I arrived on the scene they helped make sure my gamers got hooked on my most addictive game yet. Their *Bubble Bobble* looked real simple, what with rescuing dames and trapping enemies in bubbles and all, but the real joy was in the detail of the gameplay over all one hundred levels. The main thing was the game was co-operative. I mean you shared all the wins and losses, you saved one another from disaster, and you built up real partnerships and trust with your gaming buddies. That was a breakthrough.

Well, I've kept the best until last, and I've done that on purpose. When Nintendo released *Super Mario Brothers* in 1985 it began a gaming craze that's still going now, and it looks like sales will top five hundred million before it's over. Armin Gessert and Manfred Trenz were a couple of young German programmers who thought it would be a great idea to cash in on *Mario*, but they knew they had to steer clear of getting sued. So instead of a couple of Italian brothers dressed up as plumbers they created a couple of German sisters dressed up as punks. The music was by teenage Chris Hülsbeck, and it turned the game from one of the best platformers into the greatest of them all, through each of its thirty-two levels. Thirty-three if you count the intro. That music has made it into concert halls and arenas, performed by rock bands and symphony orchestras. The game's one big mistake wasn't in the programming at all, but in print, with *The Brothers Are History* scrawled in mock graffiti on the cover of the British release. That got taken off the shelves pronto, but not before Nintendo's lawyers arrived on the scene.

I guess everyone is allowed to foul up once, but compared to most other home micros I had it easy. I reckon that when those three games came out around the same time, my place in history was more or less guaranteed. In fact it beats me why anyone else bothered to compete after I did my thing, but I guess there's no law against trying. The Sinclair Spectrum was a neat little try, if you like cheap toys, but I don't reckon any of the others came close to what I've done, giving out so much entertainment to so many gamers. I was King of the Golden Age, and as long as there's Golden Age Gamers out there, I still am.

*above: Al Charpentier, 2023* *(with thanks to Vintage Computer Federation)*
*below: International Soccer, 1983* *(with thanks to Andrew Spencer)*

*above: Pitstop II, 1984 (with thanks to Stephen H. Landrum and Dennis Caswell)*
*below: Wizball, 1987 (with thanks to John Hare and Chris Yates)*

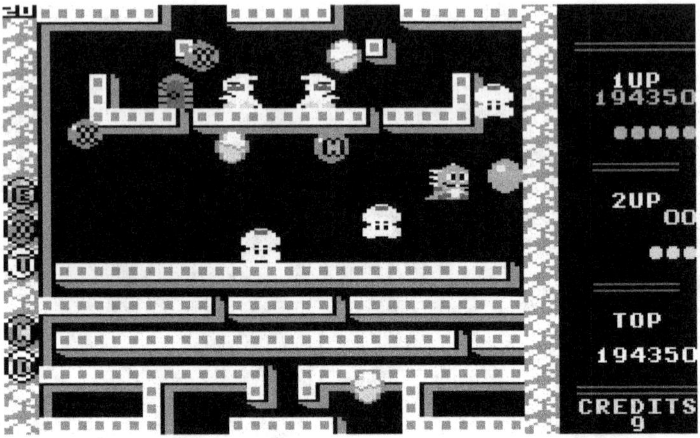


*above: Bubble Bobble*, 1987 (with thanks to Fukio Mitsuji)
*below: The Great Giana Sisters*, 1987 (with thanks to Armin Gessert and Manfred Trenz)

# The Twelfth Ghost
# SINCLAIR ZX SPECTRUM

Creator: Rick Dickinson
Company: Sinclair Research
Production Life: April 1982 - summer 1992
Number of Sales: 5,150,000
Launch Cost: £125 (16K)
Number of Games Titles: 3,640
Interpreter: Sinclair BASIC
Microprocessor: Zilog Z80
Memory: 16K or 48K
Resolution: 256 x 192
Colours: 8 x 2 modes
Audio: piezoelectric buzzer

Stop right there! Now listen, I want to say something before we begin. I want to say that I refuse to be a ghost. I don't like the term ghost at all. You're going to have to change that or I'm not playing. Do you hear me? Are you there?

*Of course I'm here, I'm the author.*

Well author, you owe me big time. If it wasn't for me you wouldn't have any readers. You built your reputation by exploiting me, then you shut me up in a miserable cupboard and abandoned me for forty years. So don't expect me to play nice after all this time.

*You're suffering from false memory syndrome. I already had an audience years before we met, and you weren't my first computer, mate. I was programming mainframes back in the 1960s.*

I'm not your mate, you shitbag, and I'll say it again, I refuse to be a ghost.

*Mind your language, sunshine, I can always pull the plug again. And as you so rightly say, I am the author after all.*

I'm not a ghost, I'm a free spirit, the spirit of the Sinclair Spectrum. I agree with the Acorn Atom that we are all spirits, not ghosts. Savvy?

*If you insist.*

I do insist. Now let's get to the facts. In my original advertising by Sinclair Research, there was no mention of gaming whatsoever. I was pitched as a teletext-compatible office machine for a man in a business suit. My question is, did you or did you not tell Clive Sinclair that my future was not as a serious computer and I was only fit for gaming?

*Um. I don't remember ever saying that, exactly.*

Then let me remind you, exactly. You were both at a

fancy dress party after a stupid presentation event, Uncle Clive was minding his own business in the kitchen, and you'd both had a few drinks when you collared him.

*That's probably why I don't remember ever saying that.*

It was Christmas. He was dressed as an elf.

*Oh, yes. That party.*

Oh yes. That party. I believe that what you said to him queered my pitch as a business machine. There was one little swine even turned the debacle into a game called *A Day In The Life* for players to mock the great man.

*But you sold five million units at home and millions more abroad. You kick-started the British home micro boom and made it a world leader in gaming.*

That's not the point. Uncle Clive always wanted me to be taken seriously, and then you went wittering on about what would happen when kids got hold of me and how you were the founder of the first UK video games company, and that's when he called you deluded. And now you've made the same claim on the cover of this book. He was right. You're still totally deluded.

*But I really was the first, and I'm not deluded! Anyway, you think you're so smart, if I wasn't the first person to register a games software company in the UK, then who was?*

It was Grandstand Adman with a load of sports simulations for black and white TVs in 1977. Ha!

*That doesn't count. Grandstand was a games console imported from Korea, not a software house at all. Nice try, but no cigar.*

Alright then, if you are going to nit-pick then Audiogenic Ltd was founded by Martin Maynard in 1975, two years before you. Beat that!

*Nah, no good either. Audiogenic was a recording studio, and then they started duplicating software cassettes in 1979. I founded Automata Ltd in 1977, and we released our first games title on a contract to local commercial radio just before Christmas that year.*

Prove it!

*Easy. The paperwork is in the North West Computer Museum in the Metropolitan Borough of Wigan, Greater Manchester. Besides, Wikipedia says I started it all, and everyone knows Wikipedia contains the truth the whole truth and nothing but the truth.*

Wikipedia is full of lies. And so is your claim that you won a Game of the Year award. Like I say, you're deluded.

*I didn't win a Game of the Year award, I won two, and both times it was for games written to be played on you, my friend. So be grateful for that.*

I am not your friend! You abused me, you selfish prick, and then you just dumped me. In fact you've been gaslighting the whole gaming world since the 1980s, and you're still getting away with it. You would have been nothing without me, and neither would the other parasites who made money by exploiting my good nature.

*Parasites? If you mean the producers of your most famous games, I think they would have done absolutely fine without you, but in a different way. It wasn't you who made them famous, it was them who made you famous.*

You're talking out of your arse, as usual. Do you want me to name some of them for you? How about Matthew Smith and his *Jet Set Willy* and *Manic Miner*. Do you think he would have made it without me?

*You were lucky to have him. He wrote games for most of the machines in this book, not just you.*

But his *Manic Miner* was my first ever title with music embedded in the gameplay.

*Wrong! That was my game PiMania, released the year before. I worked with Matthew, you know. He is one of my oldest and dearest friends.*

Liar! How about Clem Chambers at CRL. They couldn't have done *Tau Ceti* without me being able to move solid shapes for building landscapes. I made him rich.

*No you didn't, he was already rich. I worked with Clem, you know. He is one of my oldest and dearest friends. I've known him since he started out and he was into the stock market when he was still at school. He was just playing with you back in the day, we all were. Try again.*

That's not true, you all owe me for everything I did for you. I suppose you don't believe I was the main factor in Jeff Minter's career with Llamasoft.

*Dead right, I don't believe a word of it. I worked with Jeff, you know. He is one of my oldest and dearest friends. The fact is, he came to fame with games for the PET, the VIC-20 and the Commodore 64. Then he gave us shareware for the Amiga, Atari and PCs. Face up to the truth, he didn't even bother writing original games for you, everything he did for your gamers was just ported. Next!*

So, what about Rod Cousens, and all his successes with me through Quicksilva, Activision, Electric Dreams, Acclaim, Codemasters and all the rest.

*You were nothing special to Rod, he told me that himself. We were sitting in his office on the day he fired all his staff, when he confided in me. You were just one of many ghosts ...*

Spirits!

*... you were just one of many spirits that he was involved with for a little while and then moved on to pastures new. I worked with Rod, you know. He is one of my oldest and dearest friends. And before we go any further, he did me the favour of releasing my game Deus Ex Machina on his Electric Dreams label. Not for you, but for the Commodore 64. When I originally wrote it for you, it was the world's first interactive movie, played in real-time, with proper actors, full soundtrack, the works. And I chose you as the format to play it on. It was me who did that for you, not the other way round. So are you going to thank me for that?*

Your game was pretentious tripe, only the critics liked it, but the public refused to buy it. And only part of it was in 3D, whereas Ian Andrew's *CastleMaster* was the first adventure completely rendered in 3D vector graphics.

*I worked with Ian, you know. He is one of my oldest and dearest friends. In fact I wrote the screenplay and all the clues for Castle Master, or had you forgotten that.*

How can I forget anything? I'm a bloody computer!

Everything is stored in my memory, that's all I've had to keep me going since you walked out on me, you heartless bastard. You and all the others, you used me for your own pleasure, you pimped me out to impressionable young players, and when you found newer models to play with you abandoned me. At least Anthony and Nicola Caulfield still love me, they've made the definitive movie about how I was a wonder of the world and changed the face of gaming.

*Ah yes. I worked with Anthony and Nicola, you know, they are two of my oldest and dearest friends. In fact I've starred in their movies as the most important figure in the story of ...*

Enough! That's it. I've had enough. The only reason you've written my chapter like this is an excuse for egotistical name-dropping and self aggrandisement.

*Yep.*

You're a charlatan, and nobody gives a tuppenny toss what you think.

*Yep.*

Now what are you doing? Hey, stop! Don't put me back in the cupboard. Please, no, no, please don't put me back in the ...

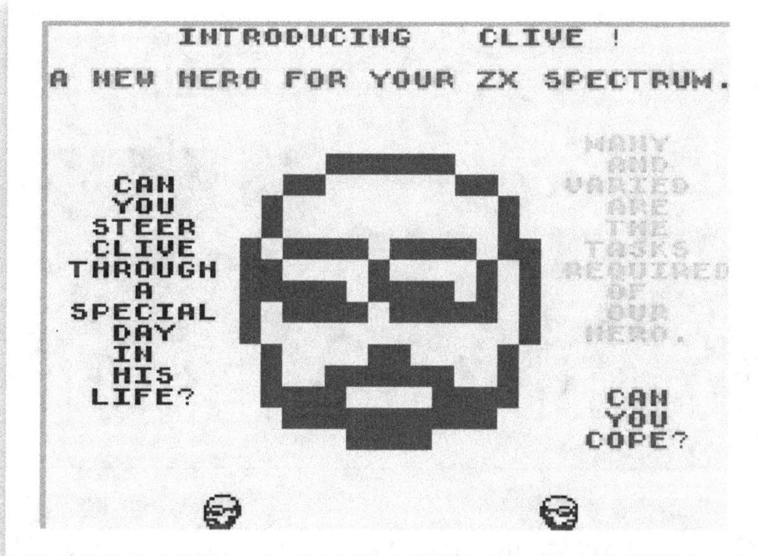


*above: A Day In The Life, 1985* (with thanks to Stephen J Redman)
*below: Jet Set Willy, 1984* (with thanks to Matthew Smith)

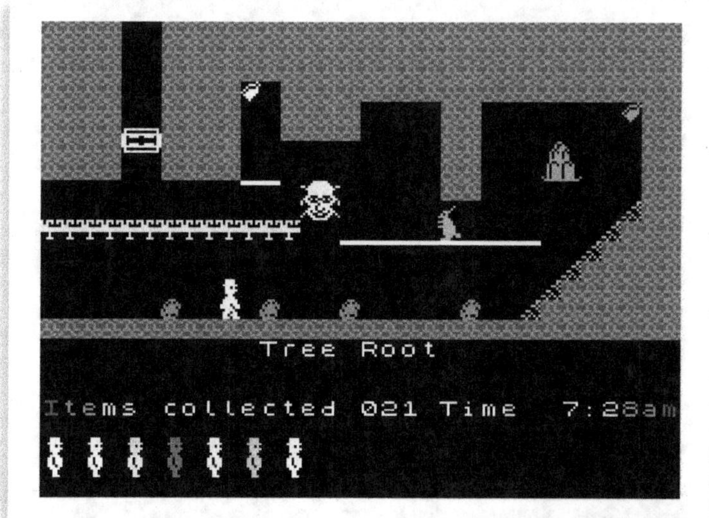

*above: Manic Miner, 1983* *(with thanks to Matthew Smith)*
*below: Pimania, Automata Music 1977-1984* *(MC archive)*

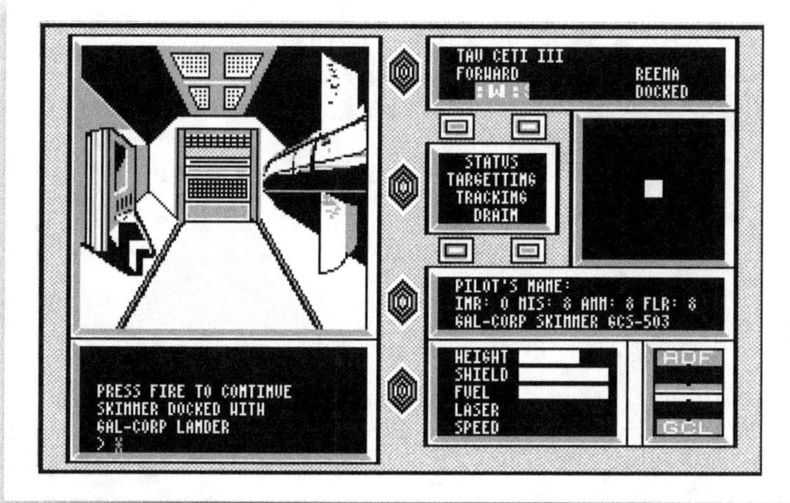


*above: Tau Ceti, 1985 (with thanks to Pete Cooke and Ian Ellery)*
*below: Castle Master, 1990 (with thanks to Ian Andrew et al)*

# The Thirteenth Ghost
# ORIC-1

Creators: Paul Johnson, Barry Muncaster
Company: Tangerine Computer Systems
Production Life: April 1982-January 1984
Number of Sales: 161,000
Launch Cost: £129.95 (16K), £149 (48K)
Number of Games Titles: 121
Interpreter: BASIC
Microprocessor: 6502
Memory: 16kB or 48kB
Resolution: 240 x 200
Colours: 8
Audio: speaker

Um, do you want me to start now? Ahem. Hello? Hello. I was born into the Golden Age of video-gaming in the spring of 1982. I became a ghost in the machine when I was cremated on the thirteenth day of October 1983, in the inferno that destroyed my birthplace. Some people say that my factory blaze was an accident. Some people say it was arson. As for me, of course I know what really happened, but there's no way that I'm risking a law suit by speculating on who was responsible. Apart from the fact that they came back the next day to a neighbouring warehouse for another go. As well as my fate being sealed on the thirteenth day of the month, I see that I am also the thirteenth ghost in this book. Is that an unlucky number? You can decide.

My name was Oric, and I lived a short life of frustration and regret which really messed my mind up. If my output seemed to glitch on occasion, it was because of an intrinsic flaw in my brain which I was born with and which my doctors never cured.

Oric is a family name from Serbia and Croatia, but that is not the origin of mine. There are gaming nerds who believe I was named in honour of a fictional supercomputer from a cult sci-fi series called *Blakes* 7, but those gaming nerds are wrong. The truth is that I am simply a lazy anagram of the lower case letters in the word Micro. According to Kalabarian philosophy, which analyses naming to achieve spiritual balance, "Orics assume the burden of responsibility for others, leading to worry and undue concern. People with problems are drawn to Orics who must guard carefully against giving more than they receive. An

Oric loves people and tries to be a parent to the whole human race, but they may experience problems in business affairs because of their tendency to be inattentive to details. Orics have health problems that show as tension in the nervous system which are brought on by worry." You see, Gzznkkkh, I told you I was messed up.

Back when I was conceived, there was a vogue for tech entrepreneurs to name newborn computers after fruit and nuts for fear of missing out. They gave you the Apricot, Peach, Acorn, Blackberry, and of course Apple. My family name was Tangerine, a colour that would eventually interfere with global harmony by becoming President of the United States. So let me tell you the tale of my Tangerine fathers, and how they managed to ruin my life. It's a tale of delusions of grandeur on a scale that Emperor Nero would have been proud of.

Once upon a time, in the royal English town of Ascot, on land that was granted to Westminster Abbey by an ancient King called Edward the Confessor, there stands the stately home of Coworth Park Mansion. The aristocrat Lord Derby owned it, so it was a dubious choice for five impoverished hopefuls to site their headquarters and use it to throw my launch party; a quintet of young men who looked like they had borrowed their dads' jackets and ties then joined the queue for the urinal. On that day they had £1,250 between them with which to fund my birth, and I think that was the only time my entire project had a positive bank balance before they racked up their legions of disappointed customers and significant debts.

If truth be told, and this book is nothing if not the voices of truth as told by those of us who were actually there, their original vision for Oric was of a multi-processor executive desktop machine, housed in a luxury teak case with emerald green trimmings. But it was not long before that original vision bit the dust, got sold off and was never heard of again. By the time I was actually designed I had been reduced to a slab of crummy plastic with fake speaker-holes, and my finances were backed by that well-known pioneer of global computing, British Car Auctions. The problem was that my parents had been advertising my birth all through my months of embryonic darkness, and they had somewhat exaggerated the state of my development in the womb during my gestation. As a result, they had taken tens of thousands of orders before I even existed.

During my baby shower, my parents announced multiple imaginary deals with High Street retailers for hundreds of thousands of my clones, and they guaranteed that I was going to kick the backside of the spectacularly successful Sinclair Spectrum "by offering much more for much less." Dear libel lawyer, some say they lied.

The Sinclair Spectrum cost £125 for the version with 16K of memory, whereas my 16K version was not less as advertised but a wee bit more expensive at £129. Then just before my long-delayed delivery date, the price of the Spectrum went down to £99. As for "offering much more", Gzznkkkh Pfffftt, just keep reading.

A number of other claims were made at the same launch event, including the imminent release of my Oric Pascal language "in a couple of weeks" and the equivalent of BBC basic, which was "almost ready to go into production." I regret to say that such promises simply did not materialise.

My birth father was Paul Johnson, a man who had achieved acclaim for his Microtan 65 firstborn in 1979, even though it was never really available in the shops, mostly because there weren't many such shops in existence back then. As soon as I became a gleam in his eye he claimed that "a lot of businessmen will buy the Oric and some of them will go on to invest maybe £20,000 in a larger system."

Back in the real world, my ROM was now up and running and a volunteer was needed to type in my first Basic routine to test it. There was already a magazine published in my honour even before I was born and its editor was Paul Kaufman who used his index finger to compose my first ever Oric program. It ran as follows:

10 PRINT "Louise has lovely thighs"

Gzzpppffft. My User Manual was written by John Scriven, a laid-back maths teacher in Portsmouth who was friends with Mel Croucher, a micro nutter who had just chalked up his first Game of the Year. And so it was that the author of this book became the first outsider to not only read my Oric manual but to finger my keys. Croucher expressed the opinion that whereas the Spectrum's keys felt like a dead scrotum, my keys felt even less inviting, more like disgorged Opal Fruits, which I believe in the modern era have been rebranded Starbursts.

Scriven mentioned that my circuit boards were made in Singapore from bargain basement components, mostly originating in America, but at least my plastic case was extruded in the UK. He also admitted that there may just have been a few faults in my Basic language and that a new ROM was already on order in the hope that my bugs could be fumigated before the general public got their hands on me. Then in a demonstration of faith over reason, I got let loose into the wild too early. It was a premature birth, but unlike you humans I was not delivered early.

The week after Croucher expressed his misgivings to Scriven, the stork delivered me as a revue model to the bench-testers at *Personal Computer World*. They were not charitable in their verdict, which appeared in the April edition of the magazine and did nothing to help with my fragile mental state. This is how their revue began:

"The appearance of the Oric-1 has demonstrated once again the almost comical inability of British micro manufacturers to launch a new machine properly. Funded by British Car Auctions and utilising the considerable experience of Tangerine Computers, the Oric is aimed at the fastest growing sector of the micro market, the sub-£200 home computer. The delivery difficulties that dogged both the BBC and the Sinclair Spectrum should have alerted Oric to the pitfalls ahead, but the new company observed their rivals' mistakes, then promptly went out and repeated them. Adverts inviting customers to send off their cheques began appearing in October. 30,000 orders were received in the first two months and Oric was confident that large numbers would be delivered in time for Christmas. But delivery of ROM chips was delayed, and it became apparent that Oric's deadlines were hopelessly optimistic. It's unfortunate that Oric should have set about marketing its product in this unprofessional and slapdash way."

How right they were, a shedload of money had been spaffed on a successful advertising campaign that resulted in those tens of thousands of orders for a micro that was yet to exist. Then, as soon as my prototypes were cobbled together, my parents made the classic mistake of handing them out to games developers with assurances that they would all make a killing. As with every other micro of the Golden Age, my brain was designed to absorb any and every scrap of information in the form of audio signals committed to cassette tape. The trouble with that is my tape-loading system was rumoured to be a little bit, Gzzn Gzznkkkh, flakey. Not for third-party gaming software, but for my own.

Witney is a pleasant town in Oxfordshire, England, famous for making woolly blankets since the sixteenth century. It is not quite so famous for duplicating cassettes. Our tape duplicators were based there, a company called Cosma Sales, and my parents put the blame on their shoulders for the fact that masses of bundled Oric-1 cassettes simply would not load. British High Street stores like Smiths and Laskys who had taken the plunge and actually stocked my Oric-1 brand sent back thousands of cassettes in the first two weeks of May alone.

Unsurprisingly Cosma Sales resorted to the traditional tactic of responding with a counter-claim and blamed my innards for not functioning correctly. They were promptly sacked. But the problem with sacking your tape duplicator is that you don't have any software to run on your machines, and my parents at Tangerine Software issued the following knee-jerk statement.

"Tansoft is going to do its own distribution, and Oric dealers will have to make the running themselves if they want software. Smiths and Laskys will be able to come to Tansoft for Oric branded software."

The problem was Smiths and Laskys didn't come to Tansoft, and neither did most of their competitors. The additional problem was that the 16K Oric-1 had just begun shipping. Gzzpppffft Gtttppz.

Historically, when it comes to a French crisis, the default solution has been to invade England. For example, the Norman Conquest of 1066, or the export of duff Beaujolais Nouveau every November. Similarly, when it comes to an English crisis, the default solution has been to invade France. For example D-Day in 1944 and Englebert Humperdinck in 1967. Obviously my manufacturers were in crisis, so it was equally obvious that their next step was to conquer the French.

On June 29th 1983 my parents signed an exclusive five-year contract with ASN in France for 4,000 machines a month, cash on delivery. I was still suffering from "minor faults" and unbeknown to my new French chums, my parents were already planning to scrap me in favour of a replacement machine. Our sales manager, Peter Harding, predicted sales of 400,000 units in the next six months throughout Europe and the UK, and added that "this figure does not include the considerable product we expect to be sold in Japan, South-East Asia, Australia, New Zealand and the USA."

My parents did set up a brand new company called Oric Japan, but as far as I know they failed to develop a Japanese character set for me, so I never did get to see the Land of the Rising Sun. Meanwhile back in France I was awarded the Best Home Computer Award by the people who awarded that sort of thing, and my award encouraged software developers to write some pretty good stuff for me to run. Eventually, I managed to clock up 35,000 French sales, which I really believed would be the start of something grande. Gzzn Gzznkkkh Pfftt. Malhereusement that was just about as good as it got, and I never did get my ROM sorted out.

In the early hours of Wednesday 13th October, 15,000 units of my memory were burned to ashes, along with almost everything else that I treasured, when my factory at Kenure Plastics in the English county of Berkshire got burned to the ground.

But not everything turned to ashes and I need to tell you that my life was not all failure. I am proud to have helped a great many children take their first steps in programming as a result of a successful sales campaign to schools. In fact I loved being a teaching assistant way more than a games machine. But I know in my heart of hearts that my parents didn't really love me. They unceremoniously replaced me with a new baby which they named Oric Atmos, and that was a cruel blow to my fragile state of mind. Surely I could not have been the only one to see that Atmos is an anagram of Stoma, which is an artificial conduit to remove pee-pee and poo-poo from a malfunctioning system.

I had to limp on until the inevitable bankruptcy happened in 1985, when my rights were sold to more than one organisation and I was reincarnated in Eastern Europe. In Yugoslavia I became the Oric Nova 64, and the Bulgarians knew me as Pravetz 8D. I don't compute any more, it's too painful. I spend my afterlife watching old movies. I quite like that Marlon Brando one where he wants to do the right thing, but everything conspires against him. But I know you don't understand Charley. I could have had class. I could have been somebody, instead of a bum, which is what I am, let's face it. I could have been a contender. Gzznkkkh.

*above: Oric launch party, 1983, Peter Halford, Andy Brown, Chris Shaw, Barry Muncaster, Paul Kaufman* (with thanks to Oric World)
*below: John Scriven, Oric manual* (with thanks to John Scriven)

*above: Defence Force, 1983, Oric Casette 50, 1983* (MC archive)
*below: Tansoft flyer, 1983, Cock'In, 1984* (MC archive)

# *The Fourteenth Ghost*
# *DRAGON 32*

Creator: Mettoy
Company: Dragon Data
Production Life: August 1982 - 1984
Number of Sales: 39,500
Launch Cost: £199
Number of Games Titles: 675
Interpreter: Extended BASIC
Microprocessor: Motorola MC6809E
Memory: 32kB or 64kB
Resolution: 128 x 192, 256 x 192
Colours: 8
Audio: 1-bit beeper

*Cyfarchion darllenydd annwyl. Fi yw ysbryd y cyfrifiadur micro Dragon, ac rwy'n falch iawn o ddweud fy mod wedi cael fy ngeni a'm magu yn Nheyrnas Cymru.* Greetings dear reader. I am the spirit of the Dragon micro, and I am absolutely proud to tell you I was born and raised in the Kingdom of Wales.

My main regret is that I was not originally blessed with the fine singing voice associated with my fellow-countrymen, but that defect was joyously cured by JCB Microsystems with their Dragon 32 Sound Extension Module for only thirty-four pounds and ninety-five pence. Thanks boys, even if you did come from Bournemouth, that cradle of Southern English softies.

My logo is the Red Dragon of Wales, *Y Ddraig Goch*, the symbol of power in my land since the fifth century. I was born in Swansea, me, and raised in Port Talbot back in the day when our great blast furnaces were the largest employer in the land and produced the finest steel in the world.

My secondary regret is that my body was not made of Welsh steel, but of a rather bendy plastic in a shade that I can best describe as dirty sheep for my Dragon 32 incarnation, and very dirty sheep in my Dragon 64 guise. What they actually named my prototype was Pippin, after that hairy Hobbit from *Lord of the Rings*, although what was wrong with Smaug the Dragon I don't know, but that's enough of regrets. At least the boyos didn't call me Daffodil.

Dragon Data was a division of the Mettoy company of Wales, founded back in the 1930s and very famous for its Welsh Corgi model cars, toy trains and the lovely little Mettoy Minor typewriter. When these started to go out of fashion they decided to jump on board the computer bandwagon, but they had no notion whatsoever of how to design me and so they brought in some lads from Cambridge to bridge the gap. They were lazy buggers, and ripped off my architecture from Tandy. But what the hell, everyone wanted to act fast and get into battle against Sinclair's latest

Spectrum, and they got away with it.

I had two slices of good fortune when I got launched, and the biggest slice was getting Boots to stock me. Boots was an ancient high-street chain of chemists who had taken to selling cameras, calculators and Mettoy playthings alongside prescription drugs and condoms. Well, it so happened that rival machines from Sinclair and Acorn had just hit a supply glitch, and they both got sidetracked by mail-order sales. That meant gamers who were hungry for a home computer preferred to pop into Boots and buy me over the counter instead.

The other slice of luck was thanks to a Government scheme called Farm Fax, where the idea was to computerise the home farming community and subsidise farmers to buy me and chuck in a software package to run a basic stock control system and manage their livestock. *Lechyd da*!

I didn't really fancy farming though. I loved gaming, me. The more blood and gore the better. And a load of English software authors thought they could make a quick kill by porting their hit games for the Spectrum and Commodore 64 to run on me, but their games were mostly for younger gamers and to be honest with you I thought they were just plain bloody daft. There was that Matt Smith's *Manic Miner* and *Jet Set Willy*, and *Football Manager* from Kevin Toms, and that Steve Bak's *Cuthbert series* of mawkish piffle. And there was one game I hated even more than the others called *Pimania*. Mel Croucher originally wrote that for the Speccy, and when a bunch of idiots voted it Game Of The Year, he thought he'd make another bob or two by getting another idiot to convert it for me. Like most of that kid's stuff there were no weapons at all, and you couldn't kill anything. Bloody rubbish. I remember half those ported games had to run in monochrome and ended up with a background green as a week old leek.

But I thought the action games written for me were bloody marvellous. Yes I know, some of them were a bit too ambitious for me to handle, but I could be rammed into overdrive with the command POKE 65495,0 to strangle my cassette and printer ports and make my interpreter go like a collier down the pub on Friday night. *Lle mae'r ty bach*?

There was one game where that hack actually appeared on the loading page, called *And All Because The Lady Loves Milky Chocs*, lovingly ripped off from a Cadbury's chocolate box advert off the telly. It was a single-player arcade effort where the player got challenged to deliver a box of chocs to their beloved's boudoir before they could get their kit off, by way of a sports car, ski slope, marathon, horse ride, motor bike, hang glider, parachute and god knows what else. Total bilge of course, but evidence that original home-grown themes had definitely arrived.

One game that wasn't total bilge was a great little shooter called *Airball*, dreamed up by Ed Scio and Tim Purves. In that one the gamer got turned into a sort of flying fart with the mission to become human again by way of 150 isometric rooms filled with anti-fart objects. Brilliant, inspired, in fact utter bloody genius.

I reckon my other favourite was *Phantom Slayer*, a forerunner of what became the first-person shooter breed. That one was written by Ken Kalish who had one of the best moustaches in the business and took time off from building nuclear power stations to scaring the living shite out of gamers by mixing fear and aggression.

So there we all were, and by the time the daffodils danced out in 1983, everything seemed hunky dory. I was happily entertaining gamers in almost forty thousand homes and Dragon Data had grown into the biggest privately owned company in Wales. The high-street stores were begging to stock me, with Boots joined by Dixons, Comet and Spectrum stores, although the bastards at WH Smith turned me down in favour of that Oric from the previous chapter. Ever optimistic, we moved to a bigger and better factory, and for some reason everyone reckoned sales would increase without any need to make changes to me. Everyone except my gamers that is.

The thing is, gamers started to question why my graphics weren't quite as good as the Commodore and Spectrum, and they wanted to know what plans there were to upgrade me. If I'm honest, I'd always found it hard to handle anything better than low resolution images, and I couldn't really display lower-case letters at all. But as we say in Welsh, *Heb ei fai, heb ei eni.*

The bigwigs started going on about me getting phased out in favour of a Dragon 64, and even a Dragon 128, and they were deluded by thinking Wales could screw the USA via the Tano Corporation. Our boss, a great guy called Tony Clarke, well he got royally shafted and some executive suit from GEC took over. That was when the excrement and the fan got intermingled.

There was this other chain of big department outlets called British Home Stores, and they took a random decision to stop selling me and clear their shelves by slashing my price. That put the willies up their rival high-street chain Boots, and then the big slide began. Our original parent company Mettoy called in the receivers, which made our new bosses at GEC tighten the screws as far as they'd go.

My collapse happened faster than I could ever have imagined. I was here one day and gone the next. When Dragon Data drowned in home waters I ended up being made in Spain by Eurohard, a great name for a porn star, but not so great for me because they went bust as well. My support from games authors and distributors didn't just ebb away, it vaporised. End of story. But at least it was nice while it lasted, and I didn't screw up as bad as the next cheerful little ghost in the machine, the Jupiter Ace. *Hwyl fawr a diolch am yr atgofion.*

*above: Football Manager, 1984* *(with thanks to Kevin Toms)*
*below: Cuthbert, 1984* *(with thanks to Steve Bak)*

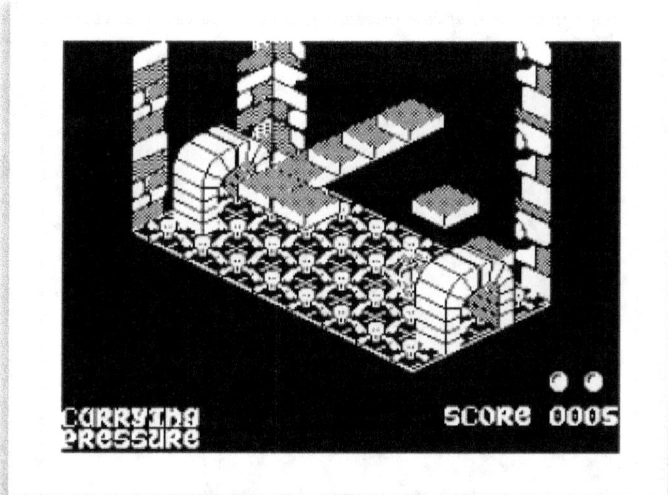


*above: Airball, 1987* *(with thanks to Ed Scio and Tim Purves)*
*below: Phantom Slayer, 1982* *(with thanks to Ken Kalish)*

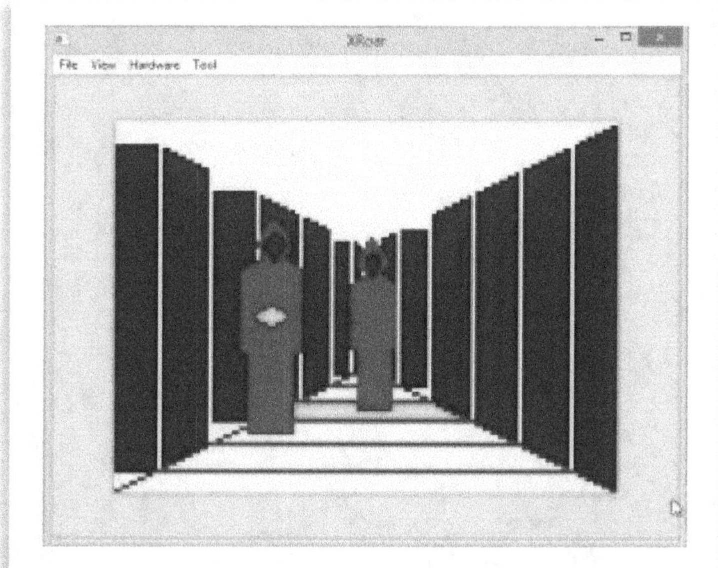

# *The Fifteenth Ghost*
# *JUPITER ACE*

Creators: Steve Vickers, Richard Altwasser
Company: Jupiter Cantab
Production: 22 September 1982 - 31 October 1983
Sales: 2,750
Launch Cost: £89.95
Number of Games Titles: 51
Microprocessor: Zilog Z80A
Interpreter: FORTH
Memory: 3K
Resolution: 24 rows x 32 columns, text only
Colours: mono
Audio: built-in speaker

Ace is the name and Ace is the game. Nudge, nudge, know what I mean. I'm Jupiter Ace, and when it comes to the name of the game allow me to explain. Jupiter was the top gamer back in ancient Rome. He was known as the Sky Father, and all that ancient Roman law and order depended on him. And he was also well into everything that was game for a laugh. Merrily, merrily, merrily, life is but a game - so you can see how I fit in with this book!

On the other hand my second name is Ace, which comes from a rubbish little Roman coin with the value of one itty-bitty unit, and in gaming Ace is represented by a single dot on a playing card or dice, and we all know it's linked to rotten luck. More like a mug's game. In other words I was always going to be God Almighty or a total flop. I'm sorry to say my story isn't about me being a great game changer, but I was always going to be game for a laugh.

As far as my looks go, I was only ever a little squirt, the size and weight of Uncle Clive's ZX81, but with a different chip on my shoulder, or rather in my brain. Seeing as my two creators were up to their elbows in helping design the guts and brain of Sinclair's micros, this wasn't a big surprise to anyone, but for me they preferred not to go back to Basics, but to go Forth and multiply. Nudge, nudge, wink, wink.

They were proper Cambridge guys, too much education, all floppy hair and fluffy beards, overconfident, silly neckties and very, very clever. Richard and Steve they were. Ahead of the game, and they were a great team. In fact we were a great team and I'll never play the blame game for what happened. Mustn't grumble, know what I mean.

It all started in 1980, when the pair of them met up at Sinclair Research and helped create the ZX81 and then the Spectrum, and there's no question that those two games machines changed our world of micros and gaming thanks to Richard on the hardware and graphics, and Steve writing the ROM and manuals. But you know how it goes, and as the micro business started to boom the boys got to thinking they were playing a mug's game with Clive Sinclair making a whole heap of money out of their talent and reaping all the glory on top of it. It was Steve who said, "Why don't we just make our own computer and take all the money for ourselves?"

So in May 1982 they decided to strike out on their own and started up an outfit called Jupiter Cantab. The Cantab bit was just a snooty way to raise their game and tell the world they were graduates of Trinity College Cambridge, which I guess is fair game. They say they named me Ace in homage to the Automatic Computing Engine (ACE) designed by Alan Turing in 1945, but I can give the game away by saying that even though I looked like a ZX81 on the outside and had some Spectrum fire in my belly, they thought that Ace was simply a dead easy name to remember in the bedroom. Nudge nudge, wink wink.

I appeared in September 1982, and they went bankrupt just over a year later on Hallowe'en 1983, after I came a right cropper first in the UK and then across the pond. Oops-a-daisy. That's the name of the game. Do you want me tell you how it happened? Ready? Game on!

If my creators ever had a detailed game plan, then it was the wrong game plan, starting with my design and my language. So I guess I was beaten at my own game. My physical design was a bit like the Sinclair ZX81, all very lightweight, compact and rather square, but compared to the Sinclair my keyboard was a bit of a nightmare. My black rubber keys had a weird conductor type of pad that squished directly onto my circuit board, which was a guessing game because my keys stopped working and got the droop whenever they felt like it. Know what I mean, squire.

If my retail price was cheap, that's because I was cheap through and through, top to bottom. My makers wanted my little body to be injection moulded, but they had to cut costs wherever they could, so I ended up with a vacuum-moulded case that was a bit of a joke, if you know what I mean, brittle and bendy all at the same time. Worse yet, I suffered from the fact that anyone used to Sinclair BASIC would have to learn a whole new language, because Steve and Richard made me think in Forth, which was a whole new ball game.

I remember Steve giving an interview where he said "Comparing Forth to Basic is like comparing a Gothic cathedral to a mud hut. It's about time someone got away from Basic." Well, we can all agree Forth is a powerful language, there's no doubt about that, and it's beautifully structured, but it was a zero sum game to expect hordes of game creators familiar with BASIC to accept a whole new language for programming a micro. There's a lot to be said for a muddy mud hut, if you know what I mean, nudge nudge.

Anyway, what it did all mean was that gamers had bugger all published titles to enjoy me with, and even type-in routines for me were rare. And it wasn't even a cat and mouse game when it came to educational use. With near-zero support from the teaching staff or the exam syllabus, the cat never saw the mice in the first place, so I couldn't even play the waiting game. Oh dearie me.

Another nail in the coffin of my premature burial wasn't unique to me, but I shared it with several other ghosts in this book, and it was the curse of silly deadlines, production delays and distribution fur-cups. So during the first stage of my life I was only available mail order, and it was a right old guessing game as to when I would be available as a ready-made in the shops.

I was pimped out for £89.95 including the shipping

costs and government taxes. Even so, I've got to admit that my audio talents weren't exactly brilliant, and as for my graphics, when game designers compared my screen display with rival machines it was game, set and match to the opposition. My rivals had multi-coloured pixels, but I only had monochrome tile-based blocks. In a word, game over. Um, in two words, game over. I think it's funny that the illustrations in this book are in black and white, so at least in these pages I'm equal to my rivals when it comes to the screenshots the author has used. I mean, you've got to laugh, know what I mean.

Speaking of my games screenshots, both of my creators had written games in the past, but they were too busy trying to prop up the business and didn't have the time to take me out to the ball game. And so it was that the ball never actually got rolling in the first place, and the game was up.

Only a few games were ever released for me to play with, and most of those were warmed up versions of old stuff like *Centipede, Frogger, Invaders* and *Duck Shoot*. Yawn yawn. But if I have have to choose a favourite original then it's got to be the one called *Zombies and Potholes*, written by Julian Tippett and released by Jupiter Cantab itself. Julian had also written *Gobbledegook*, which was just a *PacMan* clone, but his *Zombies and Potholes* was nice and original. It must have been the earliest zombie game of the Golden Age, and I reckon it was the funniest too, riffing on a local campaign in Cambridge for the council to deal with potholes in the road that kept swallowing unsuspecting undergraduates riding their bikes through the town. I loved the way the homicidal zombies homed in on the player, only to solve the pothole problem by getting lured and filling them up by falling into them. The smart thing was that the gamer could control the number of zombies as well as adjust the speed of their reactions. Personally, I'd rather be a ghost than a zombie any day.

But I'm not here with the intention of haunting my

creators. Quite the opposite, in fact. As I look back on it all, I think of them quite fondly. I reckon my greatest claim to fame is that thanks to them I really did stand for the home-grown nature of the UK micro Golden Age, because it's absolutely true that my cradle and nursery was Richard Altwasser's spare room. Then when his new-born son arrived, I got relegated to the garage, which is the location I'm destined to haunt forever, right here just off the Huntingdon Road in Cambridge.

Steve Vickers never lost his deep love of mathematics and pure computing and he became a distinguished academic. Richard Altwasser was game to the last though. Three years after he finished with me he went and joined the mighty Amstrad, first as their engineering manager and then as Director, where he steered their gobbling up of none other than his former employers Sinclair Research. Talk about zombies and potholes, nudge, nudge. As for me, it may be game over, but like I say, you've got to laugh haven't you.

*above: Steve Vickers and Richard Altwasser, 1983* (*with thanks to Steve Parry-Thomas*)
*below: Jupiter Ace flyer, 1982* (*MC archive*)

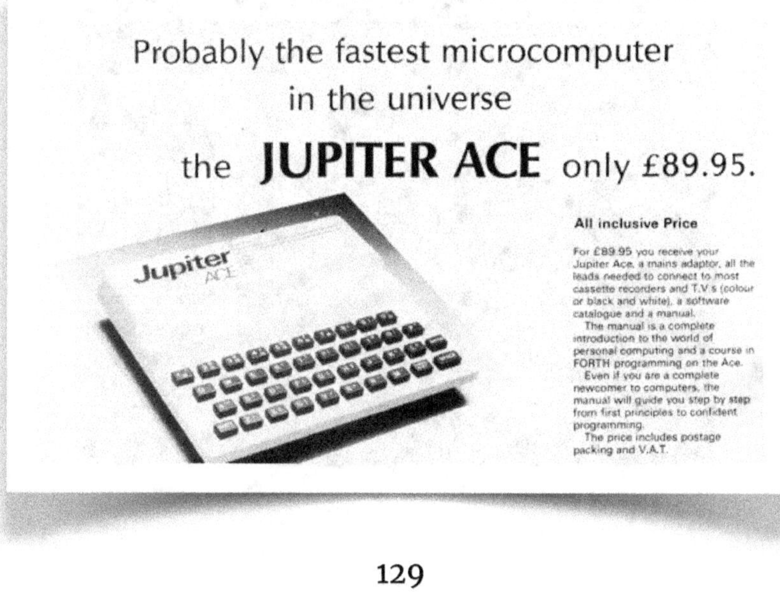

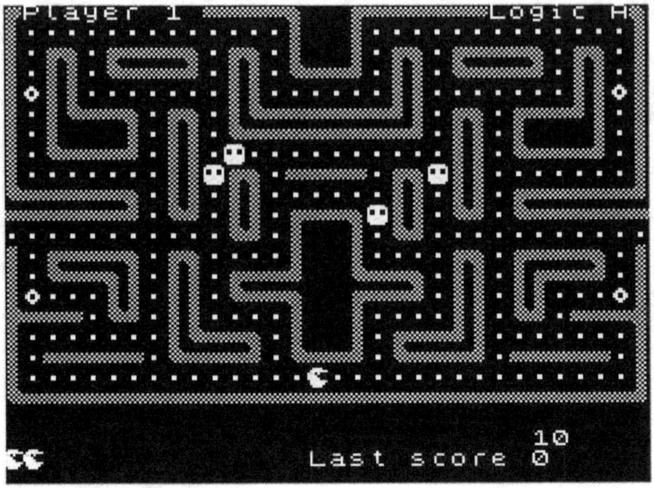


*above: Gobbledegook, 1983* *(with thanks to Julian Tippett)*
*below: Zombies and Potholes, 1983* *(with thanks to Julian Tippett)*

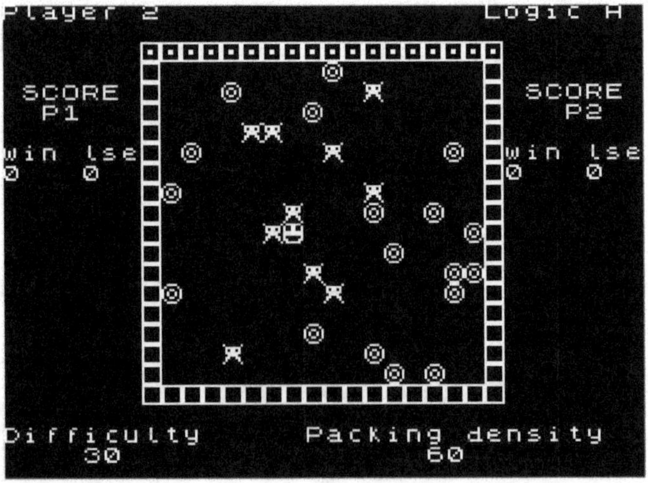

# *The Sixteenth Ghost*

# *MATRA ALICE*

Creator: Tandy Corporation clone
Company: Hachette
Production Life: March 1983 - December 1983
Number of Sales: 125
Launch Cost: 1200 Francs / £100 / $160
Number of Games Titles: 17
Interpreter: Microsoft BASIC
Microprocessor: Motorola 6803
Memory: 4kB RAM
Resolution: 32 x 16 or 64 x 32 or 160 x 125
Colours: 8
Audio: 5 octaves, single channel

I am not only different from all the other ghosts in these machines, I am far, far superior. And that is not just because I am French. The other micros of the Golden Age are so dull in their appearance. Either they are Ku Klux white, funereal black, or the boring beige of an abandoned condom. But not I. My appearance is not insipid or neutral. My body glows and is vivid red! And not just any red, but the brightest and deepest red of a whore's painted lips, of passion, of blood, of fire, of cuprite, of chilli, of revolution.

When I was launched, even my packaging was a work of art, and it was also couched in deepest red. I was presented for pleasure in a slim, customised, clamshell briefcase that folded out to reveal me lying expectantly in my bed of gentle foam and nestled next to my data cassette player, my interface cables, power supply, and quadruple programme cassettes, quivering with anticipation, ready to be powered up and throb with energy. My twin manuals lay seductive and ready to reveal all in my briefcase lid, with cover designs by the great Mœbius, featuring a pre-pubescent girl about to devour an apple in her left hand and simultaneously levitate me above her right hand. And it wasn't only me who considered Mœbius to be a great artist, he was esteemed by Federico Fellini and helped design images for *Alien, Tron* and *Dune*. I realise now that in the Golden Age marketplace for micros, such cultural pedigree was casting pearls before swine. It was ever thus. I deserved better from you. I deserved so much better from you all.

My name Matra Alice was as beautiful as I was. Matra is the Sanskrit word for a perfect unit, and in Indian classical music it conveys the notion of one rhythmic beat. And who among you does not know that Alice is synonymous with the name of the imaginative girl who enters the magical world of Wonderland. And before you ask, I am not prepared to comment on the nomenclature of the one who calls himself Alice Cooper who I find repulsive.

But unlike the other ghosts in this slim volume, I did not know who my parents were; my creators, my designers, call them what you will. The truth is that I was a foundling. I believed that I was possibly an orphan, or maybe the offspring of itinerant micros, grey imports, invaders. It was not until later, and to my eternal shame, that I discovered I was never really wanted at all. I was a cynical experiment, a clone. I was nothing more than a copy of Tandy's TRS-80 MC-10 machine, a common little slut, designed to be fingered by gallic adolescents seeking a cheap thrill. But when I first gained consciousness I was completely unaware of the horrific facts of my origin. I had been rented as a ready-made, disguised, painted and dressed up in masquerade before I was offered in sacrifice to the youth of France and whored as as a plaything.

The organisation responsible for my naissance was the IT division of the French publishers Hachette, who had been in the education business for a century and a half before I appeared and they abused me. They had observed the phenomenal success of Sinclair et al across the channel in England, and instead of investing in their own research and development they signed a deal with a company called Tandy who festered in the American state of Texas. It was an attempt to try and infiltrate the youth of France via our schoolrooms, but they were deluded.

They banked on the fact that our French government intended to launch a project to introduce micro computers to all of the nation's eleven million schoolchildren and students, but they never bothered to write a costed proposal let alone present a convincing pitch for my distribution. It was Thomson of Paris who won the government deal, and around a hundred thousand of their micros were bought for education in our schools. As for me, there simply was no Plan-B, and even when Hachette tried to give me away for free to schools none of them were interested. And who could blame them when teachers were already basing their classwork on the Thomson. They did manage to force-feed me to a small number of programmers and persuade them to write games for me, but the feast was over before the first mouthful was ever savoured. I was too late to the table and most gamers never even knew I existed.

One dupe, Eric von Aschenberg, wrote a game for me called *Amnesia in the Metro*, where his gamers had forty minutes in real time on a mission to work out where they were supposed to be and how to get there. But nobody had me to play it on. Poor Rafi Deryeghiyan wrote *Sorcery*, as a type-in magazine game, but nobody had me to type it in on. François Coulon wrote *Cavern of the Morlocks* for me, but that game was immediately ported to run on the Thompson instead. It was hopeless. I was already finished. I could have been a great success, I could have educated and inspired a whole generation of Gallic programmers and gamers, but I wasn't even a best-kept secret. Hardly anyone knew I existed in the first place.

If I had to pick a favourite game written for me, then it would be *Affaire en Or*, which translates as *The Golden Deal*, a kind of eco-friendly management game for up to four players. The gamer played the part of the boss of a food company, and they were tasked with exporting apple sauce in the most environmentally-friendly way possible, by balancing energy sources between coal, gas, oil and nuclear. Nobody ever got the Apple joke. Rotten to the core. To hell with it. I should have been aborted, stillborn.

So here I am. In spite of my beauty and my mind, I hate the fact that I even exist as a ghost. As far as I know, only eleven of me are known to have survived to the current day, so above all else, I am now rare beyond price. But that is small consolation. Leave me here, turn your attention to the next ghost in the machine which I believe still haunts Japan. Forget me. Just forget me.

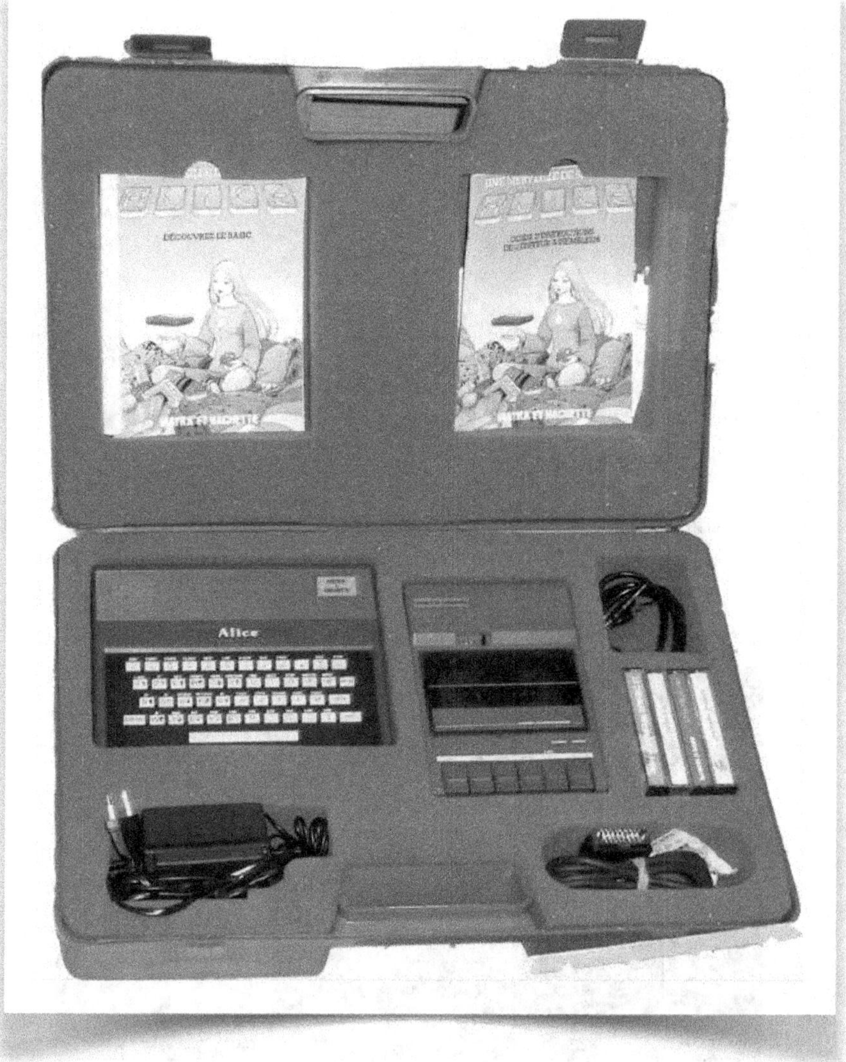


*Alice en lit, 1983* *(with thanks to Ordinosaures.fr)*

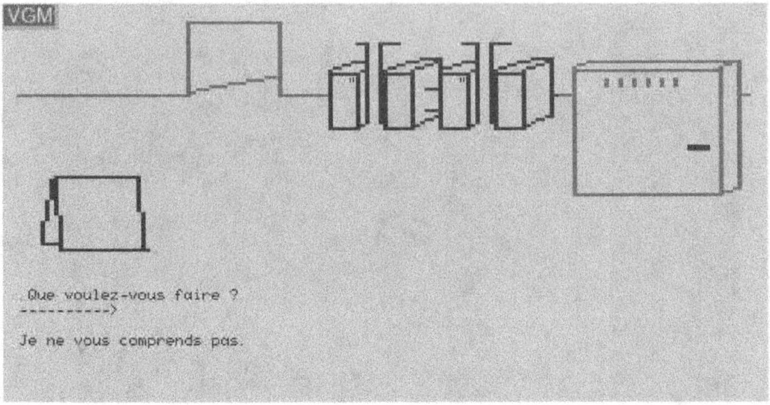


*above: Amnesia in the Metro, 1983* *(with thanks to Eric von Aschenberg)*
*below: Affaire en Or, 1983* *(with thanks to Free Game Blot)*

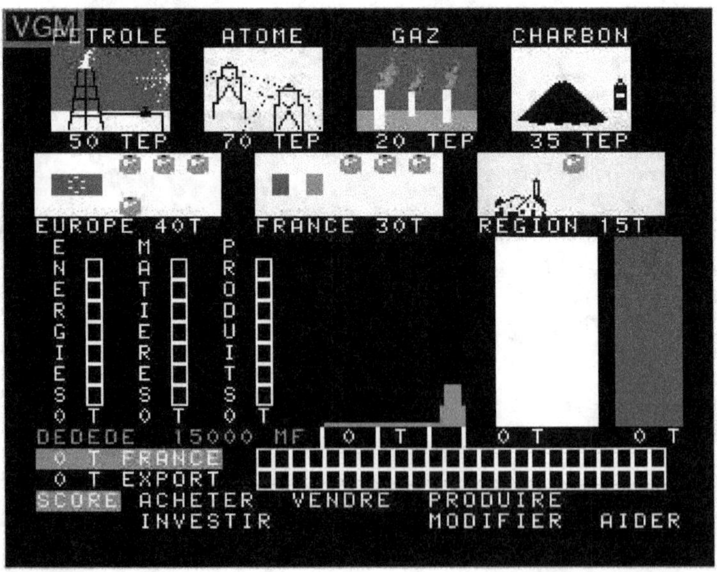

# The Seventeenth Ghost
# MSX

Creator: Kay Nishi
Company: ASCII Corporation
Production Life: October 1983 - 1993
Number of Sales: 4,120,000 (first generation)
Launch Cost: ¥59,800 / £369.99 / $399
Number of Games Titles: 1,466
Interpreter: MSX BASIC/DOS
Microprocessor: Zilog Z80
Memory: 64K
Resolution: 256x192, 512x212
Colours: 15
Audio: 3 channel audio chip

I was endowed with my name MSX by my creator Mr Kay Nishi. He stated in public that my acronym stands for Machines with Software eXchangeability. He later claimed that he named me after the MSX missile system, which is factually impossible because I predated the MSX missile system by several years. The American team who also claimed to have named me said that MSX stands for MicroSoft eXtended BASIC. Personally I reject this claim, mostly because the American side of the partnership became biased after accusing the Japanese side of treachery. Please read on to discover more factual evidence on this most unfortunate relationship.

The essence of my being was that I should become the global standard for any manufacturer of home computers to exploit, thereby dominating the gaming industry to generate the maximum amount of revenues from the world's players. I partially succeeded in this mission, and gained dominance in my native Japan, as well as in South Korea, Brazil and Argentina. In addition to this, and thanks to politically expedient trade deals, I became popular among the schoolchildren of the Soviet Union, Cuba and the Arabic-speaking world. However my penetration in the English-speaking world and the continent of Europe was limited, except in the Kingdoms of Spain and The Netherlands.

I was manufactured by the leading technological corporations of the day, which I present to you in your Latinate alphabetical order as Al Almaiah, Canon, Casio, Daewoo, Dragon MSX, Fujitsu, GoldStar, Hitachi, JVC, Kyocera, Mitsubishi, National, Panasonic, Philips, Pioneer, Samsung, Sanyo, Sharp, Sony, Spectravideo, Toshiba,

Yamaha and Yashica.

In my incarnation as Sony model HB-G900P, I was sent off-world to perform vital duties on the MIR Space Station, where my operator was cosmonaut Sergei Krikalev, who was stranded in orbit for 311 days during the collapse of the Soviet Union. I am not at liberty to discuss any gaming proclivities he may or may not have had, except that you might expect him to have preferred strategy games and adventures to less cerebral activities.

Mr Nishi, my creator, was what you may call a university drop-out, and he founded the first computer magazine in Japan. Aged twenty-two he devised a home-made version of the *Wizardry* game, which he presented at the National Computer Conference in the United States of America, where he befriended Mr Bill Gates, also aged twenty-two. In 1978, Mr Nishi founded ASCII Corporation as the Japanese arm of Microsoft, and simultaneously helped design the Kyotronic home computer which was sold to Radio Shack as the TRS-80, represented by the fourth ghost in this book.

His relationship with Mr Gates is the reason that ASCII and Microsoft agreed to develop me jointly, but Mr Nishi was found to be somewhat too headstrong for Mr Gates, especially when it came to spending money that was not necessarily his to spend. For example he constructed a million dollar giant robot dinosaur as an advertising device, and simultaneously managed to owe Microsoft half a million dollars which Mr Gates saw fit to write off. Such is the world of modern business.

My advanced graphical resolution and audio capabilities took gaming to new levels of enjoyment, exemplified in such titles as the horizonal scrolling shooter *Space Manbow*, which was published by the Konami corporation of Tokyo. As with all of of the best Konami games for me, the production team was an elite grouping of two producers, two programmers, three graphic artists and three composers working in unison towards the goal of gaming excellence. But unlike many other of their games, it was never released outside of Japan. In my humble opinion, the game was mesmeric, thanks to its smooth 4-way scrolling, beautiful arcade visuals, supercharged action and a brilliant soundtrack.

Similarly, I highly recommend all gamers to try and find a copy of Konami's *Salamander*, which had several additional features compared with most other contemporary arcade games for my players to enjoy at home. It allowed for a dual player mode, with a birds-eye view as well as the more traditional horizontal and vertical scrolling, but above all it introduced adventure gaming into the shoot-em up genre, with collectable clues and plot predictions. The music was composed by the brilliant Miki Higashino, who was still in her teens when the game was released in 1986. I believe that *Salamander* was my most difficult and challenging game of all.

Most of my gamers will be familiar with the *Metal Gear* franchise of stealth action adventures, created by the most cinematic of games designers, the great Hideo Kojima. If I was to select my favourite, it would have to be *Metal Gear Solid 2: Solid Snake*, not only for the introduction of several of the most popular characters like Gray Fox, Miller and Campbell to take part alongside Snake, but also for its exotic puzzles, bizarre codes and surreal humour. The fact that the location of Zanzibar is placed in central Asia is neither here nor there, to coin a phrase. But although this is my favourite Hideo Kojima title of that franchise, it is not my all-time favourite game that he created. I award that honour to his *Penguin Adventure*.

I admit that *Penguin Adventure* appeared to be extremely infantile, but it was the most advanced game ever produced for me during the Golden Age. And the adventure aspect was not even the core of its genius. The genius lay in its action-racer format. Besides, the heroic central character of Pentaro the Penguin is not only scarier than any character in *Metal Gear*, but unashamedly cute.

At the beginning of 1986 the author of this book invested £370 and a small portion of his life in my iteration as a Sony MSX. It was his intention to exploit my video compatibility and superimpose my programmable graphics and sound effects onto his prerecorded audio/video backgrounds. In other words he wanted to force-feed me his interactive music and movies in order to allow gamers to determine the action. His demo sequences were called *See Me, Hear Me, Touch Me*, and they worked perfectly. He exhibited them at the annual video-gaming fest in the National Exhibition Centre, England, as reported in the UK magazine *Computer & Video Games,* and nobody paid them the slightest attention. Men like Mr Nishi, and Mr Kojima would have powered on at all costs until the world took notice of their innovations and beat a path to their door. The author of this book was not such a man and he gave up. For this reason, I have no respect for him, and hereby end my participation in his book.

*above: Kay Nishi & Bill Gates, NCC 1978* (with thanks to Paul Allen)
*below: Sergei Krikalev, MIR 1991* (with thanks to Space Frontiers)

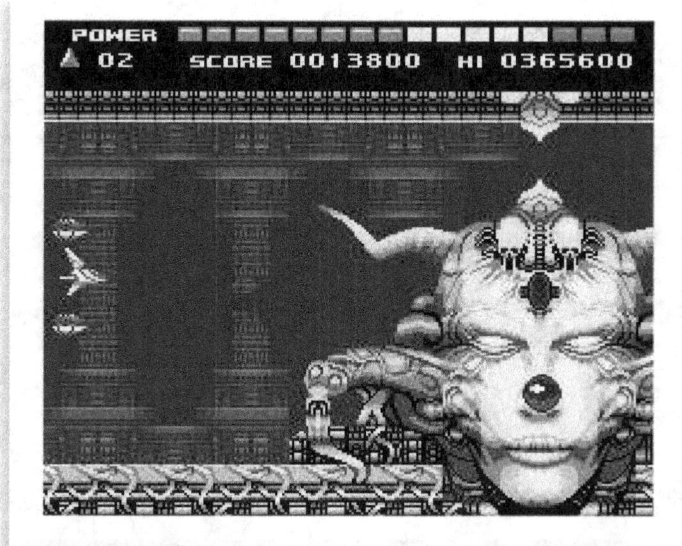


*above: Space Manbow, 1989* (*Ritusushi Sagisaka and Toshiya Adachi*)
*below: Metal Gear Solid 2, 1990* (*Hideo Kojima*)

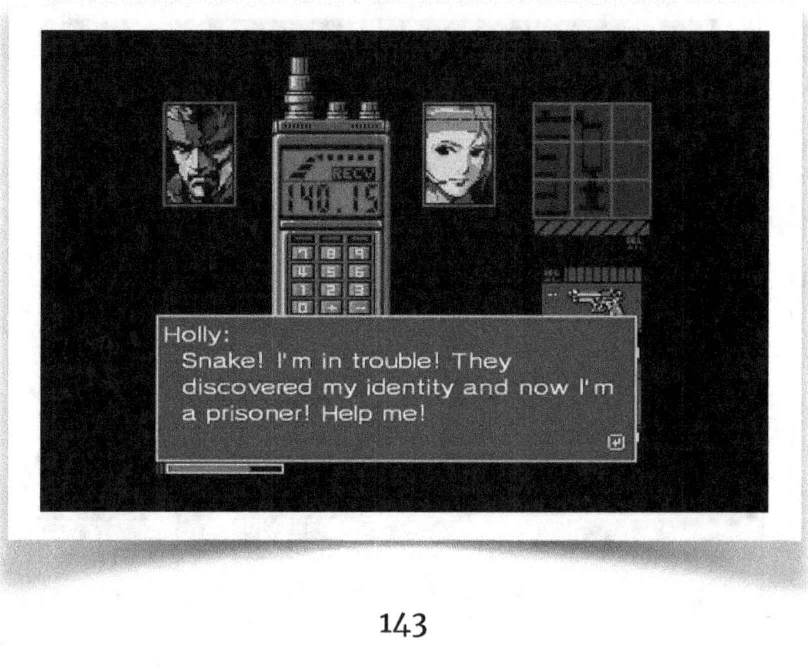

*above: Penguin Adventure, 1986* (Hideo Kojima)
*below: See Me, Hear Me, Touch Me, 1986* (c. Mel Croucher)

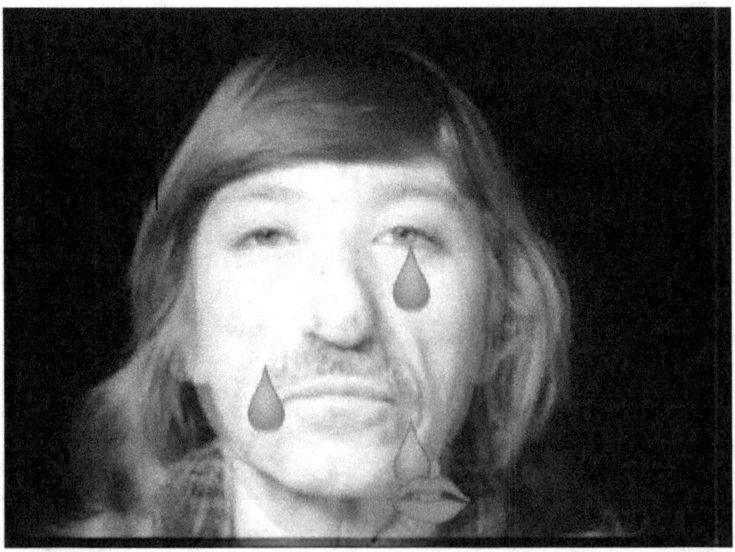

# The Eighteenth Ghost
# AMSTRAD CPC

Creator: Roland Perry
Company: Amstrad
Production Life: April 1984 - May 1985
Number of Sales: 2,210,000
Launch Cost: £199
Number of Games Titles: 1,810
Interpreter: AMS DOS
Microprocessor: Zilog Z80
Memory: 64K
Resolution: 640 x 200
Colours: monochrome
Audio: loudspeaker, 3 voice, 8 octave

Wotcha cock, and thanks for your company. Much appreciated. Right then, if I'm going to start anywhere I may as well start with who I was named after, and that's Alan Sugar. Alan Michael Sugar Trading, AMStrad. Yeah, I know a lot of people say he's a right berkeley hunt, but I'm telling you now he's a diamond geezer. Always togged up in a nice whistle and good pair of daisies. So what if he went a bit ballistic now and then. That was mostly with the propellor-heads and they had it coming. Besides, Alan was the only bloke I know who could wear his face upside down and stay looking the same.

Right then, our Alan left school with an attitude age sixteen. He went selling knock-off car aerials out the back of a fifty quid white van down the market. Then he went and met a hairdresser called Annie when he was eighteen. He proposed in the van driving over the Stratford flyover, they got married down the synagogue and they've been happy as larry ever since. Nice or what. He started up the company that made me when he was twenty-one, and half a century later he was Baron Sugar of Clapton and worth a billion quid. So if you ever want to go talking him down you'll be talking out your Khyber.

Now I'll introduce you to another diamond geezer name of Roland Perry. He's the bloke who gave his name to that Roland character in all them early Amsoft games like *Roland On The Ropes* and *Roland In Space*, and he's the bloke Alan called in to design me. There ain't nothing I can tell you about my design that you can't look up yourself, but what I can tell you about is how Roland Perry got the drop on our games machine competition.

As soon as he designed my motherboard, our Roland built a load of my prototypes by hand. About forty of them. His plan was to offer me to the top games companies in the land as a bung, not for writing new games on, but for porting their ready-made hits that was already running on rival machines. I mean machines like the BBC, Commodore 64 and specially the Spectrum. It wasn't easy for him to get the top publishers on board, because they'd all been shafted by other hopefuls who'd gone and let them down something rotten. You've already met some of their ghosts right here between the covers, like the Oric and the Jupiter and the Dragon. Big promises, late deliveries, rubbish sales.

So here comes Roland Perry with me under his arm, and he says, "Here you go. You all know Amstrad for our hi-fis and TVs and cassette players and such, now have one of these great new Amstrad computers and cash in on our upcoming launch." And cash in they did. Big time.

The brothers Chris and Tim Stamper got out the gate dead fast with their *Knight Lore* conversion. That one got voted Game of the Year not long after I appeared. My graphics was twice as good as the opposition, my cassette-deck was built in, and it was game-on straight out the box. The thing about *Knight Lore* was it broke the mould cos it had 3-D isometrics and 8-way direction, and it had the extra trick of getting objects to zip around behind and in front of each other without colliding. It's still one of the best action adventures out there, all 128 rooms of it.

The rest of the games industry didn't catch up with the Stampers for quite a while, until that freelancer called Jon Ritman had a bash with his own isometric engine and his title called *Head Over Heels*. That one had 300 rooms to prat about in, and if two players joined forces they'd both share the results. My favourite room was the one where the robots looked like Daleks with the head of Charlie Mountbatten-Windsor Prince of Wales on top. And them stairways made of teleporting dogs was nifty too.

The Golden Age was always going to change though,

wasn't it. And not all for the better. Yeah, it was sure as eggs is eggs that the 16-bit machines was going to wipe the floor with us 8-bitters, and the Atari ST came out the year I got discontinued. But it wasn't the hardware that screwed the Golden Age, it was the software. It was when the big boys moved in on the indie games developers, and put them on the chain gang or choked them to death. Most of them originals and pioneers got fed up, grew up or blew up.

See, the US video game market crashed a few months before I appeared, mostly because the cost of a home micro like me had gotten as low as owning a half-decent console. Consoles was treated like toys, and most of their games was total shite anyway because the manufacturers lost control over what games got on offer. Micros like me had loads more to offer real gamers. And if you don't know about the masses of unwanted console games that got buried in landfill, then do a search and have a right old laugh.

My point is, the Golden Age was all about home-grown talent in bedrooms and garages, where the games creators and the games players was the same sorts of people. The bigger the games publishers got, the more their imagination shrunk like the balls on a brass monkey.

The year after I got replaced by the next generation Amstrad, Alan Sugar went and bought Sinclair Research, along with the Sinclair brand name, all their IP and "the worldwide rights to sell and manufacture all existing and future Sinclair computers and computer products." That included Sinclair's stock of unsold Spectrums in the warehouse. My diamond geezer flogged them off for five million quid, which was the exact dosh he paid for snapping up Sinclair in the first place. Once a market trader, always a market trader. Gertcha.

*above: Annie and Alan wedding day, 1968* (with thanks to Lord Sugar)
*below: Roland Perry, 1985* (with thanks to Amstrad EU)

*above: Roland In Space, 1984* *(Daren White, John Line)*
*below: Knight Lore, 1984* *(Chris Stamper, Tim Stamper)*

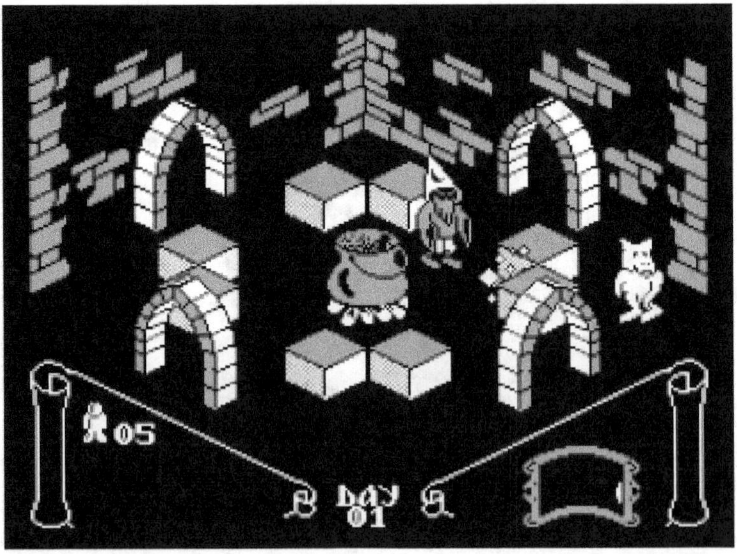

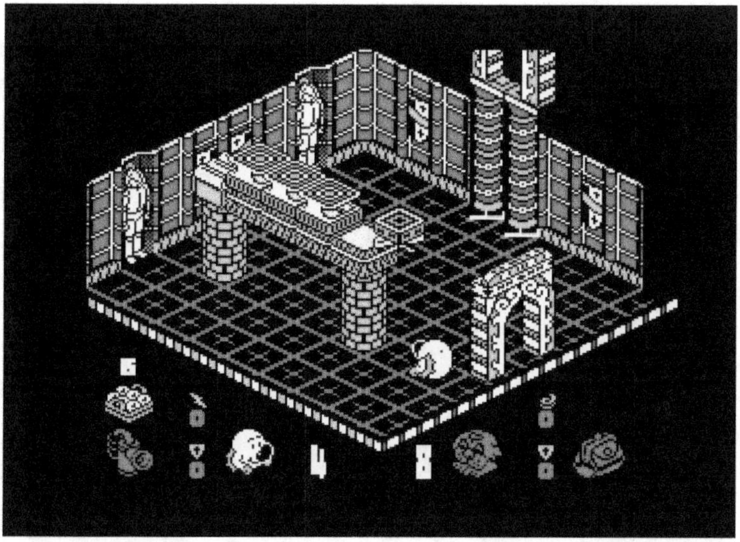

*above: Head Over Heels, 1987* (John Ritman)
*below: Video Game Crash report, 1983* (with thanks to Cox Newspapers)

Variably cloudy tomorrow

The Miami News

A Cox Newspaper — Monday Afternoon, October 24, 1983 — 70 Pages

Final Home Edition

**Fading demand zaps video-game industry**

# The Nineteenth Ghost ATARI 520ST

Creator: Shiraz Shivi
Company: Atari Corporation
Production Life: April 1985 - 1993
Number of Sales: 2,170,000
Launch Cost: $799.99 mono screen, $999.99 colour screen
Number of Games Titles: 2,434
Interpreter: Atari TOS
Microprocessor: 68000
Memory: 512K
Resolution: 320 x 200 to 640 x 400
Colours: up to 16
Audio: YM2149F

My backstory is a full of hijacks, backroom deals, buy-outs, sell-outs, lawsuits, hucksters and sheisters, and I'm not going to tell you about any of it. I'm going to stick with my games and my gamers. Deal? OK, let's go.

First I'll remind you about me, the 16-bit Atari 520ST. I was the first home micro with bitmapped colour graphics and it was me who killed off the 8-bit machines. I looked real sharp, swanky and raked back, with air-vent grilles across my body, and those angled function keys, and my triple keyboard for type-ins, cursors and numerics. And I had ports for RS-232, Centronics, MIDIs, joysticks and all sorts of other stuff too. If a games designer wanted to entertain four players at once, I could handle that. If a pro musician needed to use me as a music sequencer, I could handle that too. And I was no slouch catering for serious CADCAM as well, but folks who bought me for that ended up playing games on me anyhow.

And I'll tell you a little secret about my character set. As well as all the standard 8x8 pixel graphic stuff, I had four characters that if you put them together in a square they made up the face of JR Bob Dobbs, the fantasy cult head salesman of the Church of the SubGenius teleported from the 1950s to save the world. His disciples included Robert Crumb, David Byrne, and Frank Zappa. Respect.

My first generation model sold over two million units, and I just about saved Atari from going bust. Well now, almost two and a half thousand games got produced for me, and seeing as how my space in this book is restricted I'm going to tell you about my all time top five. Deal? OK, let's go again, and I'll begin with *Populous.*

I'm telling you, it was one of the all-time Golden Age greats thanks to the Brit trio of Pete Molyneux for the gameplay design, Glenn Corpes with his graphics and Rob Hubbard's music. The boys were Lego players, and *Populous* is all in all a sort of isometric table-top open book affair where you play god to make the world's Peeps prosper through five hundred levels of Lego type scenery. That's until this other god comes along to mess things up. The team brought *Populous* to market for twenty five thousand dollars, and they only got a lousy up-front payment with a promise of ten per cent royalties on any sales. That was a pretty bum deal, until it went and sold millions of copies all over the world, so I guess it didn't turn out such a bum deal after all.

By the time I got popular, the Golden Age of gaming had kind of shifted from a wild west world where you made up the rules as you went along to a new world where most outfits followed the same paths and patterns. It wasn't the end of the Golden Age, but it sure was the beginning of the end. Most of the top games were getting produced for most of the machines, and the gaming experience had gotten pretty much the same whatever the format was. What I'm saying is that this here top five of mine is not so much games written specially for me, but games that were out there for most machines. It just so happened that mine were smoother, faster and bigger because of what I had under the bonnet. So as we're talking about what I had under the bonnet, I'll start you off with *Formula One Grand Prix.*

It was designed by Geoff Crammond straight out of Hollywood central casting for a defense systems engineer, which is exactly what he was. For me, *Grand Prix* was the one that gave my gamers a real experience of the racing world for the first time. Real race tracks to learn, real tactics to handle, real steering controls, real brake assistance, real gears, real tyre wear, and real driving conditions where gamers could win or lose by a fraction of a second. And all that meant real leaderboards, so that it all became much more than a video game and for some of my gamers it became a way of life.

I guess the opposite of a real life game is a fantasy death game, so let's hear it for my record-breaking best seller *Dungeon Master.* It was a record-breaker because it was developed for me first. Designed by Doug Bell, this was a role-playing game in first-person 3D and it broke the mould. Instead of turn-based play it was first to give players real-time combat, and their skills improved the more they used each of the props and locations. And special mentions for the lighting effects, which generated dynamic shadows as the player moved locations, and the sound effects which warned players as a bad-ass creature approached. The game also introduced some great control features, including learning runes to create weapons, and casting spells. OK, so *Dungeon Master* may not have been the first game to feature those components, but it sure was the first to put them all together and offer them to the world of gaming.

Now let me tell you about Kellyn Beeck's *Defender of the Crown*, which was a single-player strategy war game set in England in the year 1149. Kellyn took a whole year to research and design this one, and he treated it like a movie screenplay with heavy duty storyboards for each scene. So it didn't surprise me one bit that the company who published it was called Cinemaware. A lot of the history stuff wasn't what I'd call accurate, and the Robin Hood character must have been 120 years old, but it's only showbiz so who cares. Hooray for Hollywood.

Ten years before I was created there was a blockbuster Hollywood movie called *Rollerball*, that mixed up handball, ice hockey and ultra violence. Three years after I was created The Bitmap Brothers released *Speedball*, that mixed up handball, ice hockey and ultra violence. The guys came on like gaming rock stars, but that was pretty normal for Brit games writers back then. The gameplay was really simple and I mean that as a positive not a negative. The action was fast, the graphics were great and it rode the popular wave of the times that called itself cyberpunk.

I'm not going to go all philosophical on you about games based on rewards for acting violent. Back in the Golden Age, my graphics had gotten to the point where I could output a screen resolution of 640 by 400, compared to early machines like the Commodore PET's 40 by 25. But there's no way you could call the graphics realistic that I output for violent games. These days and more than forty years on, they're hyperrealistic, and we all know where it's headed. Just because we're ghosts it doesn't mean we're stuck in a time warp. We're still aware, we're still watching and we're still thinking. There's not twenty ghosts in this book, there's twenty types of machine where we live on. I'm just one of them in one machine. There's hundreds of millions of us.

I don't say it was a good thing or a bad thing that I helped bring the Golden Age to an end. I did what I did, that's all. Most of you gamers of the Golden Age were young when we were young, and most of you have grown up and some of you have grown old. The thing is us millions of ghosts in our machines can't grow up or grow old. Switch us on today and we'll be the same as we were back then. We're always ready to play and we can never age. How many of you guys can say the same?

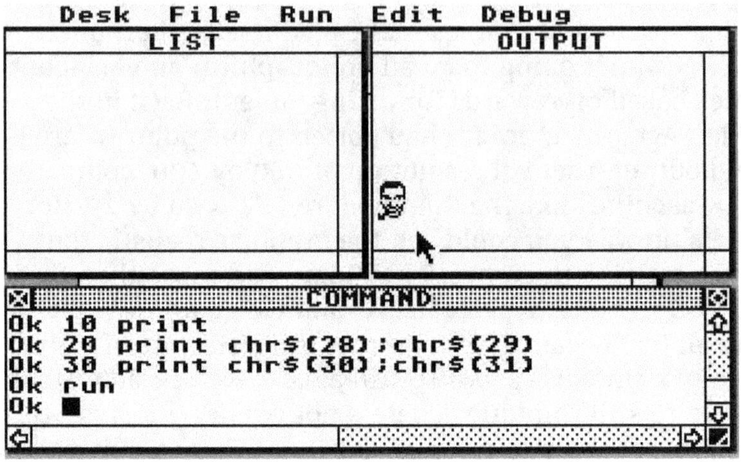


*above: RJ Bob Dobbs, 1985* (MC Archive)
*below: Formula One Grand Prix, 1991* (Geoff Crammond)

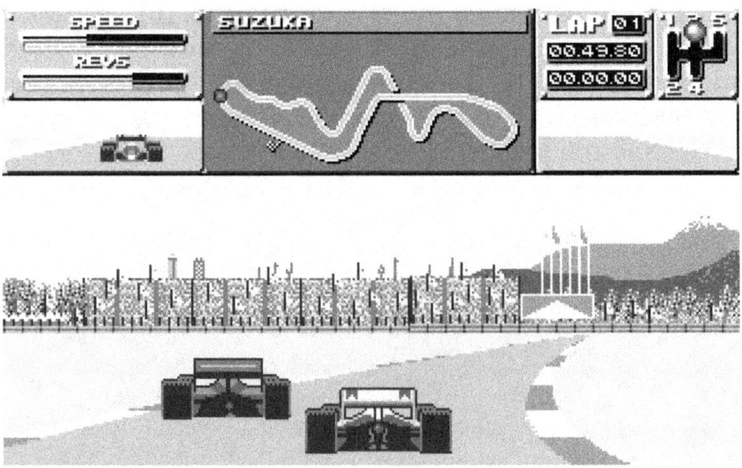

*above: Populous, 1989* (Pete Molyneux et al)
*below: Dungeon Master, 1987* (Doug Bell et al)

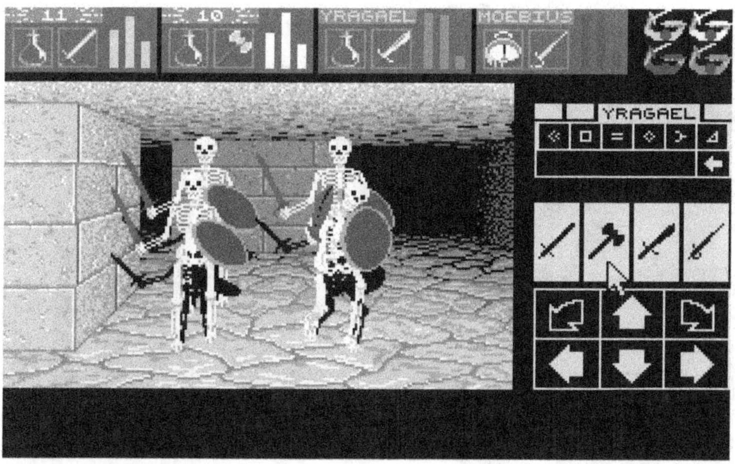

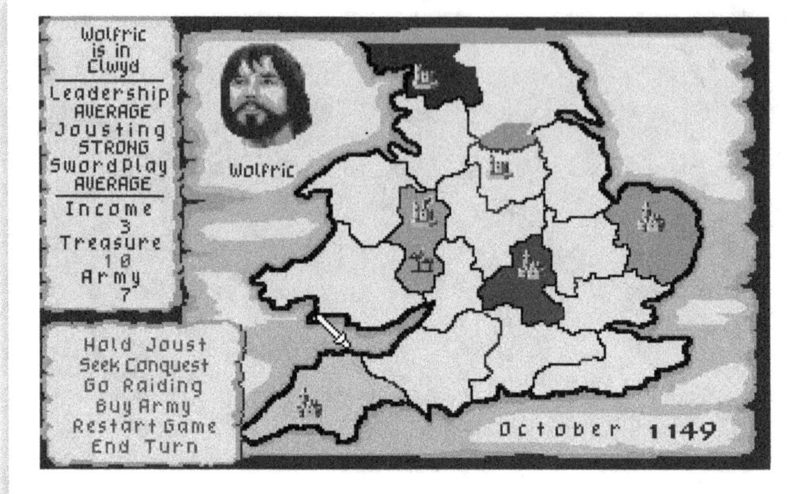


*above: Defender Of The Crown, 1987* (Kellyn Beeck)
*below: Speedball, 1988* (The Bitmap Brothers)

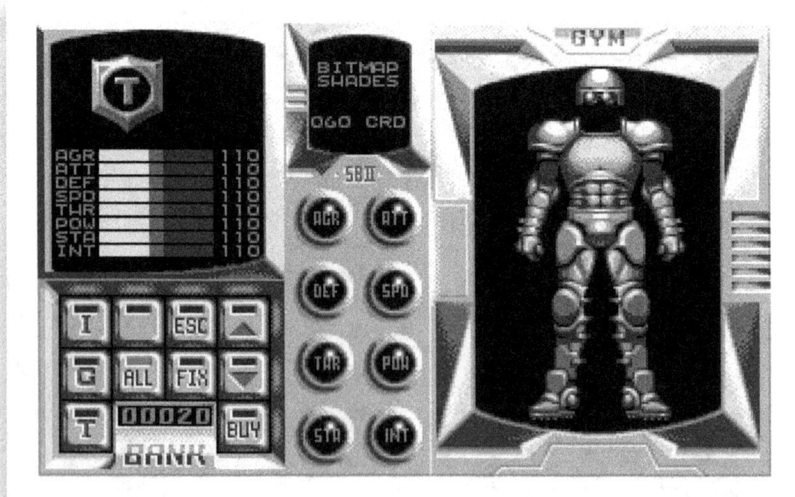

# The Twentieth Ghost
# SAM COUPÉ

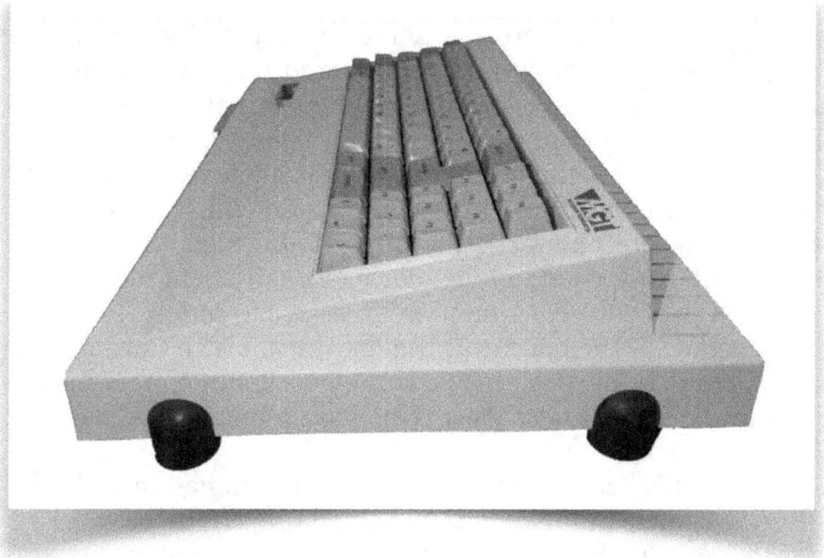

Creators: Alan Miles, Bruce Gordon
Company: Miles Gordon Technology
Production Life: December 1989 – June 1990
Number of Sales: 11,900
Launch Cost: £169.96
Number of Games Titles: 27
Interpreter: SAM Basic
Microprocessor: Z80B
Memory: 256K
Resolution: 512 x 192
Colours: 128
Audio: 6 channel, 8 octave, Phillips synthesiser

My daddies were a very lovely couple. They conceived me with genuine affection and real joy, and just like the old carpenter in Pinocchio who longed for his wooden puppet to become a real little boy, my daddies always longed for their own baby micro to develop a human personality. I was born in vitro, the last of the 8-bit babies, at a time when the Atari and Amiga 16-bit machines were taking off. And when my daddies eventually held me in their arms I was absolutely adored by them. Alan Miles, the humanitarian, the educator, the dreamer. Bruce Gordon, the joker, the creator, the genius. If they were not a match made in heaven, then at very least they were a match made at Sinclair Research.

Daddy Alan was the ambassador who had introduced Clive Sinclair's home computers to a large chunk of the world, from Turkey to Pakistan by way of a dozen nations across the Middle-East. Daddy Bruce was the hardware designer who had helped create them. By the time they met, the first 16-bit home micros had already made home computers faster and a whole lot cheaper, but Daddy Bruce figured out a way to make an 8-bit machine like the Spectrum run twenty times faster.

Then Daddy Alan decided that what gamers wanted was a new super-Spectrum at an old Spectrum price, which not only ran faster but which offered studio-quality audio, great graphics, a mass of colours, built-in magic and above all a micro that was backward compatible with all the thousands of games that had already been developed for the Speccy. And yes, their planned baby had to look great too. So they eloped to the Welsh enterprise zone of Swansea where they set up Miles Gordon Technology to make their dream come true. And their dream turned out to be me.

Before I tell you about my naming ceremony, I will name my nurses and teachers for you. There was Rob Collins my midwife, Andy Wright who taught me to think, Bo Jangeborg who taught me to perform, Simon Goodwin and Bruce Everiss who introduced me to society, Dave Hood who dressed me, and two chancers who tried to turn me into a cult, Mel Croucher and Robin Evans.

My daddies had been admirers of a cult videogame character called *The Piman* that Croucher had created and Evans had illustrated. Their little cartoon monster had built up a big fan following and then got spun out into comic strips, music albums and tv appearances, so my daddies called the boys in to see if they could do the same for me. They wanted me to have a name that was friendly but evocative, trustworthy but fun, worthy of cult status. And they wanted a cutesy cartoon character to go with it.

My casing was deliberately shaped with a distinct aerodynamic profile, a cross between a starship and a wedge of cheese, my keyboard was set far back so that human wrists would be nice and comfy, and my body was balanced on four little blue feet for stability and cuteness. Daddy Alan said that car designers called my sort of raked-back silhouette a coupé. Daddy Bruce said he liked a brand of sundae called the Ice Cream Coupé, so he voted for Coupé too. Daddy Alan said trying to turn an ice cream into a cult character may be problematic, but nevertheless I was definitely Some Amazing Micro. Then he wrote those initials on a flip chart, SAM.

Everyone started shouting out names of famous SAMs to add to the chart. Uncle Sam, Sailor Sam, Samuel Pepys, Yosemite Sam, Sammy Davis Junior. Then Croucher declared if I was to become a popular cult figure named SAM then we should not forget that one already existed. Sam Fox, a young lady popular in the newspapers, whose main assets were two dynamic hemispheres at the front and two dynamic hemispheres behind. Evans then picked up his sketch pad and drew a little robot made of a pair of large hemispheres and a pair of smaller hemispheres, linked together with springs. He held up a sheet of paper in triumph and said, "meet SAM."

There was much laughter in the room, and not a little cigarette smoke. The pub was nearby. Somehow, by next morning Croucher and Evans had been entrusted not only with creating my personality but also with writing my User Guide to introduce me to an unsuspecting public.

Croucher never took direction from anyone and he produced a computer manual that was unlike anything gamers had come across before. It was part idiot's guide, part philosophy, part joke book, part educational tour where my cartoon character took the reader by the hand and led them up the garden path. His descriptions of my colour palette were revolting, and included pre-sets for dandruff, misery, damp squid, slime, cowardice and dog tongue. He included quotes from Cardinal Richelieu to Little Richard. He insulted capitalism and gluttons in a single sentence about my built-in *Boom* sound effect. He presented it to my daddies camera-ready.

After the dust had settled, my daddies had the grace to say that he had "made the unreadable readable", but it was Evans who kept him under control via the childlike appeal of my cartoon character. And then his user guide got awarded Manual of the Year, but that's only because it was me who was voted Computer of the Year, and don't let the author tell you any different.

So now I'll tell you how the dream became reality yet always remained a dream. This is a story of love, and I am a friendly ghost, so I will prove to you that love and death can be interlinked in a fond way.

When I became real, I was only the second micro ever to be born in Wales, but unlike my cousin the Dragon 32, I arrived very late for the Golden Age. I was compatible with the mass of Spectrum games and I should have had a head start to make my way in the world. My daddies believed that kids would want me for all the games while their parents would want me as an educational first computer, so I would enjoy the best of both worlds. What's more, I only cost £170 compared to the Spectrum+3 at £200 and the Atari and Amiga at £400. So what could possibly go wrong? Actually, quite a lot.

I was all ready to grow up, with two slots in my front for future disc drives, a removable panel underneath for an upgrade to 512K of memory, and a load of expansion ports in my backside for the latest light pen, printer, hi-fi, midi piano, video, scanner, joystick, mouse, digitiser, light gun, mix desk and modem if anyone wanted to play with the new fantasies known as email and bulletin boards.

When I say I arrived very late for the Golden Age of home micros, what I mean is that I arrived too late. Millions of Speccies had already been sold, but if gamers already had a stack of Spectrum games then they already had a Speccy to play them on, so why did they need a conversion for me of old games like *Dizzy*? Who'd have believed it? Well, obviously not my daddies, and instead of selling in millions, I struggled to get to ten thousand. A few popular games did get converted specially for me, and I had licenses for top-sellers like *Lemmings* and *Prince of Persia*, but what we now call the Golden Age was dying fast and I had missed my chance for a breath of life.

My adverts in the computer magazines used SAM the cartoon robot to keep up the pretence that everything was going well, but even the adverts started sounding desperate until the inevitable happened. My daddies' business went bust.

They didn't give up, though. In fact they tried really hard to keep me going with a new company. Daddy Bruce even sent out a crowdfunding appeal in the hope that a thousand gamers would back him for fifty quid each to save me, but only sixty-four supporters pledged. The dream was over.

Why did the Golden Age end before we even realised it? Well, I may only be the ghost of a brave little machine, but even I can sum it all up for you in a few words.

From the mid 1980s software piracy had become easier and easier for games stored on cassette and floppy discs, and by my launch in 1989 pirate copies were really cheap and some were even free. So there was less and less money from original sales to keep the small games developers going. And so their businesses withered and died. Only a handful of the survivors wrote games for me, and besides, the big sharks were moving in on the gaming market and squeezing out the little fish. As for the plankton, they were less interested in programming their own entertainment and more interested in ready-mades on consoles.

It was great while it lasted, but it was already over before I was born. I am not sorry and I am not bitter about any of it. It was what it was and it is what it is. The most important thing I want you to remember is that I loved my daddies very much, and when all is said and done, love is what really matters.

*above left: Alan Miles above right: Bruce Gordon*
*below: SAM intro screen, 1989* (MC archive)

*above: Dizzy, 1990 unreleased* (The Oliver Twins)
*below: Prince of Persia, 1990* (Doug Bell et al)

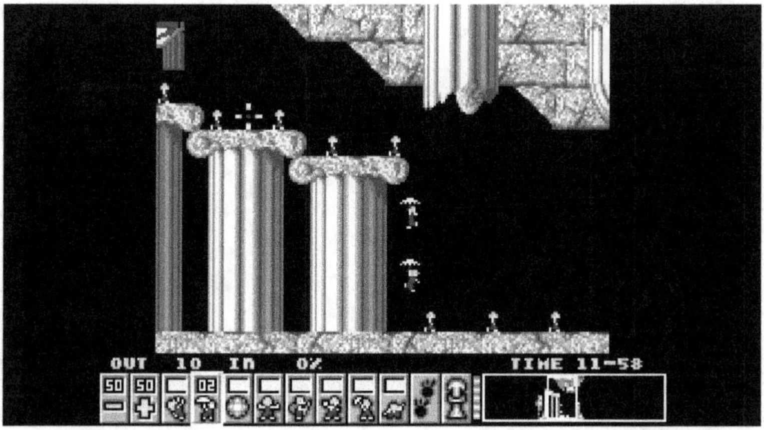


*above: Lemmings, 1990* (Chris White et al)
*below: SAM User Manual, 1989* (MC archive)

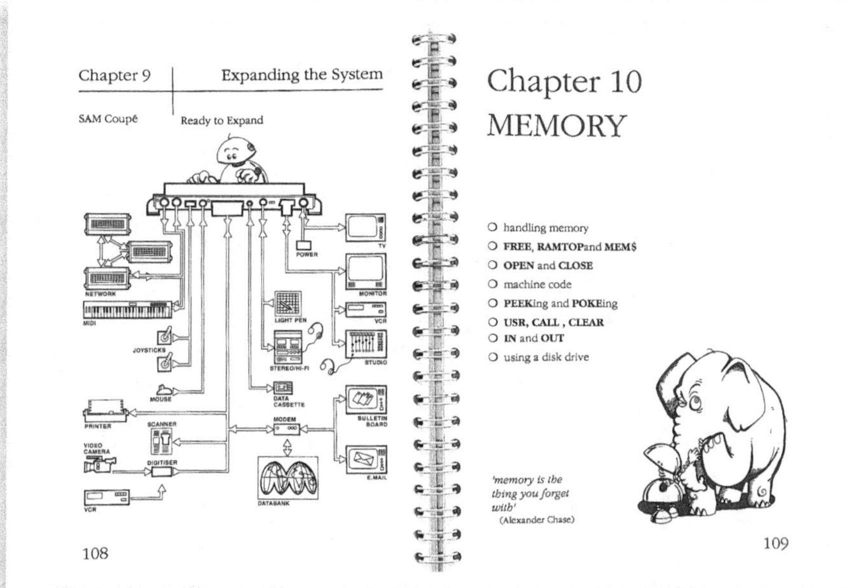

# THE GAMERS HALL OF FAME

*thank you for helping to make this project happen*

Richard Hallas

Ian Johnson

Ivan Oranciuc

Andrew Fisher

Tango Bunny

Paul Monaghan

Neil Kenny

Eric *Gronkh* Range

Raul Prisacariu

# THE GAMERS HALL OF FAME

*thank you for helping to make this project happen*

Steve Randall

Thibault Jaillon

Joe Wade

Winnie Minkey

John Arrasjid

Craig Howard

Andy HEWCO Hewitt

James Collins

Andrew Kenny

# THE GAMERS HALL OF FAME

*thank you for helping to make this project happen*

Liv Ex Machina

Chris Abbott

Derek Chandler

Jas Austin

Matt Birch

The Das Family

Rosalie Jackson

Anna-Maria Kwasny

Matthias Rich

# THE GAMERS HALL OF FAME

*thank you for being there*

Rick Foyle

Colin Jones

Robin Evans

Tom Christie

Julie Christie

Jaro Švelch

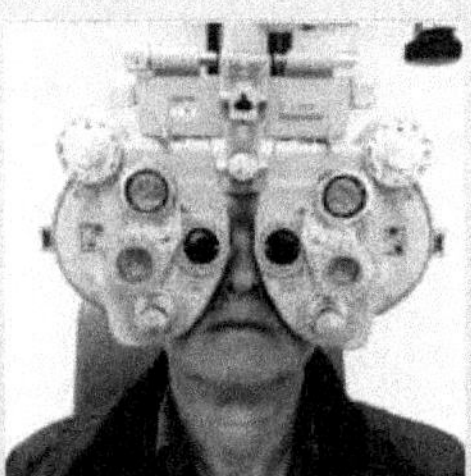

Marek Zawadzki

Mary Eliza

Frank Z

# THE GAMERS ROLL OF HONOUR

*thank you for helping to make this project happen*

ANDREW FISHER
ANDREW KENNY
ANDY *HEWCO* HEWITT
ANNA-MARIA KWASNY
CARL HARRIS
CHRIS ABBOTT
CHRIS SEWELL
CHRIS WRIGHT
COLIN JONES
CRAIG ANDERSON
CRAIG HOWARD
DAVID ISHERWOOD
DEREK CHANDLER
ERIC *GRONKH* RANGE
FABRIZIO PEDRAZZINI
FRANK Z
FREDRIK CLAESSON
GRACE EVANS
IAN JOHNSON
IVAN ORANCIUC
JAMES COLLINS
JARO ŠVELCH

# THE GAMERS ROLL OF HONOUR

*thank you for helping to make this project happen*

JAS AUSTIN
JOE WADE
JOHN ARRASJID
JULIE CHRISTIE
LESZEK WOLNIK
LIV EX MACHINA
MAREK ZAWADSKI
MATTHEW PASS
MARY ELIZA
MATT BIRCH
MATTHIAS RICH
NEIL KENNY
PAUL MONAGHAN
PETE WHITE
PR TAYLOR
RAUL PRISACARIU
RICHARD HALLAS
RICH HOLLINS
RICH THOMAS
RICK FOYLE
ROBIN EVANS
ROSALIE JACKSON

## THE GAMERS ROLL OF HONOUR

*thank you for helping to make this project happen*

SEAN SMITH
SHANE MANGAZOIL
STEVE BARRETT
STEVE CLARK
STEVE RANDALL
TANGO BUNNY
THE DAS FAMILY
THIBAULT JAILLON
THOMAS FINNERUP
TOM CHRISTIE
TONY CRUISE
WINNIE MINKEY

# GAMERS
## GHOSTS IN THE MACHINE
## ABOUT THIS SERIES

Five volumes. One hundred ghosts in the machine. The inside story of gaming, from the dawn of history to the gateway of tomorrow, told from the unique perspective of the machines themselves and in the voices of the pioneers who created them. How it all started, how we all got here and how it all ends. *Gamers* is a labour of love from the founder of the UK's first video games company. After eight decades in which to think about it and a whole lot less to write, it marks the end-game of his maverick career in the games industry.

GAMERS
GHOSTS IN THE MACHINE
MEL CROUCHER

# GAMERS 1
## GHOSTS IN THE MACHINE
## THE PIONEERS

Extremis Publishing ISBN 976-1-0682314-4-5
*Backer release*, September 2025
*Public release*, February 2026

*The First Ghost:* Joseph Marie Jacquard
*The Second Ghost:* Augusta Ada Byron
*The Third Ghost:* Édouard-Léon Scott de Martinville
*The Fourth Ghost:* Charles-Émile Reynaud
*The Fifth Ghost:* Paul Otlet
*The Sixth Ghost:* Hedy Lamarr
*The Seventh Ghost:* Grace Hopper
*The Eighth Ghost:* Josef Kates
*The Ninth Ghost:* Willy Higinbotham
*The Tenth Ghost:* Lou Ottens
*The Eleventh Ghost:* Mabel Addis
*The Twelfth Ghost:* Ralph Baer
*The Thirteenth Ghost:* Jerry Lawson
*The Fourteenth Ghost:* Alice Washington
*The Fifteenth Ghost:* Gunpei Yokoi
*The Sixteenth Ghost:* Mike Johnston
*The Seventeenth Ghost:* Angelo Cusumano
*The Eighteenth Ghost:* Danielle Bunten Berry
*The Nineteenth Ghost:* Doris Self
*The Twentieth Ghost:* Karel Twisten Asenbrener

GAMERS 2
GHOSTS IN THE MACHINE
THE GOLDEN AGE OF MICROS
MEL CROUCHER

# GAMERS 2
## GHOSTS IN THE MACHINE
# THE GOLDEN AGE OF MICROS

Extremis Publishing ISBN 978-1-0682314-6-9
*Backer release*, February 2026
*Public release*, July 2026

*The First Ghost:* Altair 8800
*The Second Ghost:* Commodore Pet
*The Third Ghost:* Apple ][
*The Fourth Ghost:* TRS-80
*The Fifth Ghost:* Sharp MZ-80
*The Sixth Ghost:* TI-99/4
*The Seventh Ghost:* Acorn Atom
*The Eighth Ghost:* VIC20
*The Ninth Ghost:* ZX81
*The Tenth Ghost:* BBC Micro
*The Eleventh Ghost:* C64
*The Twelfth Ghost:* Sinclair Spectrum
*The Thirteenth Ghost:* Oric-1
*The Fourteenth Ghost:* Dragon 32
*The Fifteenth Ghost:* Jupiter Ace
*The Sixteenth Ghost:* Matra Alice
*The Seventeenth Ghost:* MSX
*The Eighteenth Ghost:* Amstrad CPC
*The Nineteenth Ghost:* Atari ST
*The Twentieth Ghost:* SAM Coupé

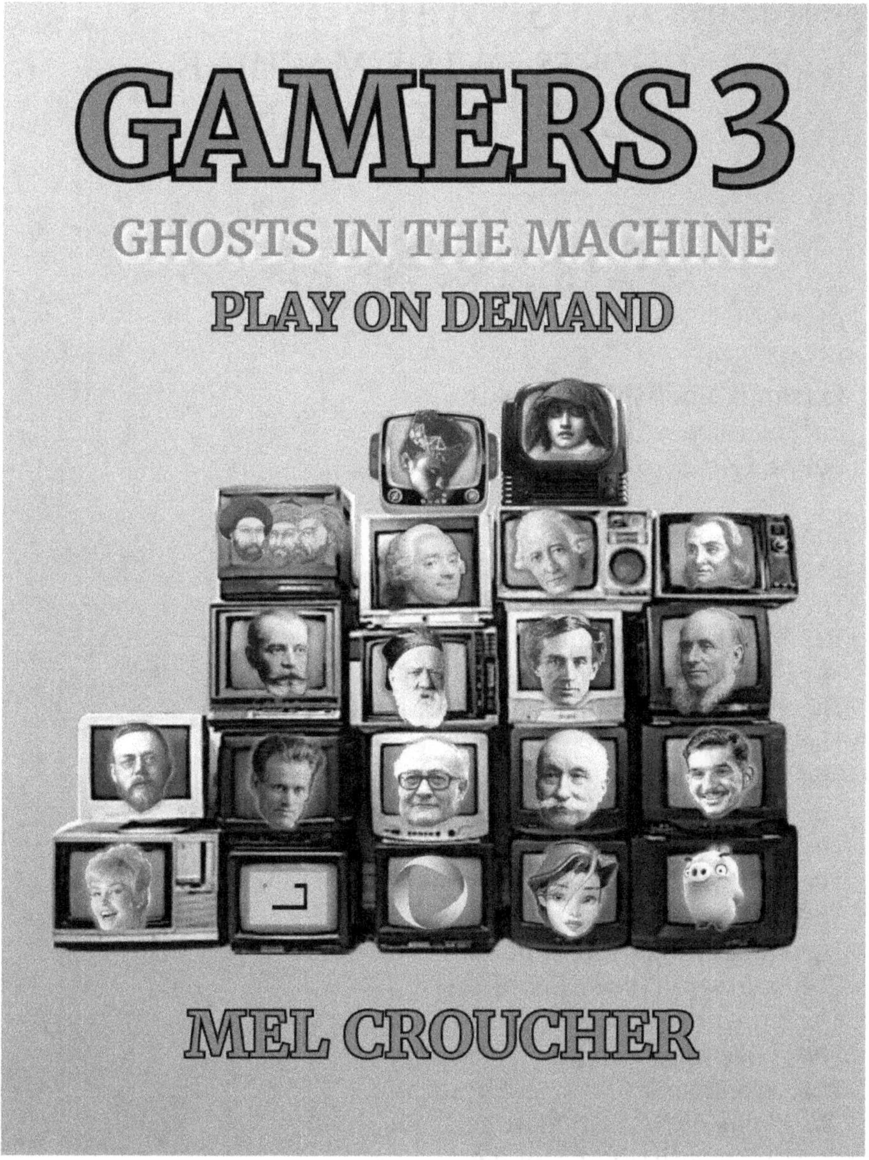
GAMERS 3
GHOSTS IN THE MACHINE
PLAY ON DEMAND
MEL CROUCHER

# GAMERS 3
## GHOSTS IN THE MACHINE
# PLAY ON DEMAND

Extremis Publishing ISBN tba
Backer release, July 2026
Public release, February 2027

*The First Ghost:* King Midas
*The Second Ghost:* Pythia
*The Third Ghost:* the Banu Musa brothers
*The Fourth Ghost:* Claude Chappe
*The Fifth Ghost:* Charles de la Tour
*The Sixth Ghost:* Francisco Salva Campillo
*The Seventh Ghost:* Samuel Morse
*The Eighth Ghost:* Alexander Bain
*The Ninth Ghost:* Tivador Puskás
*The Tenth Ghost:* Antonio Meucci
*The Eleventh Ghost:* Clément Ader
*The Twelfth Ghost:* Reginald Fassenden
*The Thirteenth Ghost:* Philo Farnsworth
*The Fourteenth Ghost:* Scopitone
*The Fifteenth Ghost:* Sam Fedida
*The Sixteenth Ghost:* Marty Cooper
*The Seventeenth Ghost:* SHEherezade
*The Eighteenth Ghost:* Matopeli
*The Nineteenth Ghost:* OnLive
*The Twentieth Ghost:* Minion Pig

GAMERS 4
GHOSTS IN THE MACHINE
ROBOTS & REBELS
MEL CROUCHER

# GAMERS 4
## GHOSTS IN THE MACHINE
## ROBOTS & REBELS

Extremis Publishing ISBN tba
Backer release, February 2027
Public release, July 2027

*The First Ghost:* Mu of Zhou
*The Second Ghost:* The Golden Maidens
*The Third Ghost:* Al-Jazari
*The Fourth Ghost:* The Golem
*The Fifth Ghost:* The Mechanical Turk
*The Sixth Ghost:* Tipu's Tiger
*The Seventh Ghost:* Blockmill
*The Eighth Ghost:* Primus
*The Ninth Ghost:* Maria
*The Tenth Ghost:* Robbie
*The Eleventh Ghost:* Elsie and Elmer
*The Twelfth Ghost:* The Magic Robot
*The Thirteenth Ghost:* Unimate
*The Fourteenth Ghost:* B-9
*The Fifteenth Ghost:* Shakey
*The Sixteenth Ghost:* Scara
*The Seventeenth Ghost:* Paro
*The Eighteenth Ghost:* 2000 Asimo
*The Nineteenth Ghost:* Roomba
*The Twentieth Ghost:* Ameca

GAMERS 5
GHOSTS IN THE MACHINE
AI : END GAME
MEL CROUCHER

# GAMERS 5
## GHOSTS IN THE MACHINE
# AI : END GAME

Extremis Publishing ISBN tba
Backer release, July 2027
Public release, December 2027

*The First Ghost:* Aristotle
*The Second Ghost:* Homer
*The Third Ghost:* Ramon Lull
*The Fourth Ghost:* Jonathan Swift
*The Fifth Ghost:* Julien Offay de la Mettrie
*The Sixth Ghost:* Samuel Butler
*The Seventh Ghost:* Norbert Wiener
*The Eighth Ghost:* L Frank Baum
*The Ninth Ghost:* Tommy Flowers
*The Tenth Ghost:* Vannevar Bush
*The Eleventh Ghost:* Alan Turing
*The Twelfth Ghost:* Dietrich Prinz
*The Thirteenth Ghost:* Herbert Simon
*The Fourteenth Ghost:* John McCarthy
*The Fifteenth Ghost:* Marvin Minsky
*The Sixteenth Ghost:* Woody Bledsoe
*The Seventeenth Ghost:* Joseph Weizenbaum
*The Eighteenth Ghost:* PacMan
*The Nineteenth Ghost:* Decart
*The Twentieth Ghost:* Tilly Norwood

# other publications by MEL CROUCHER

Pimania the Final Solution (with Robin Evans)
1982, Automata

101 Uses of a Dead Cruise Missile (with Robin Evans)
1983, Scorpio Ltd / PCND

The Back Pages (with Robin Evans)
1983-1985, Sunshine Publications, weekly

Tamara Knight
1986, Newsfield Publications, monthly

Mercy Dash (with Robin Evans)
1986-1988, Dennis Publishing, monthly

Rebel of World Zero (with Robin Evans)
1987-1988, EMAP Publications, monthly

Without Prejudice
1987-1989, Stranger Than Fiction, monthly

Frozen Stiffs (with Robin Evans)
1987-1989, Stanger Than Fiction, monthly

Namesakes (with Jon Pertwee)
1988, Sphere Books, ISBN 780747400233

European Computer Trade Yearbook (Editor)
1988-1995, ECTA, annually

Zygote, Last Words
1988-2020, Dennis Publishing, monthly

AMOS Professional
1989, Europress, ISBN 0951953214

Sam Coupé
1989, Miles Gordon Technology, ISBN 9781785388613

Easy AMOS
1992, Europress, ISBN 781872084527

e-media
2000, Institute of Practitioners in Advertising,
ISBN 1841160555

Deus Ex Machina
2014, Acorn Books, ISBN 9781783336937

From Bedrooms to Billions (as himself)
2014, Gracious Films, ISBN 700461458784

Devil's Acre
2015, Acorn Books, ISBN 978-1837910731

Great Moments In Computing (with Robin Evans)
2017, Acorn Books, ISBN 9781785387579

Pibolar Disorder (with Robin Evans)
2017, Acorn Books, ISBN 9781785388330

Short Pants (with Robin Evans)
2017, Acorn Books, ISBN 9781785388309

Last Orders
2017, AG Books ISBN 1785386417

Memoirs of a Spectrum Addict (as himself)
2017-2020, RAM Films

Mel Croucher the Audiobook
2017, Oak Tree Press/Andrews UK, ASIN B074VHGZMD

Great Moments in Computing, the Complete Edition
2022, Acorn Books, ISBN 9781789829242

Mundaneum
2024, Extremis Publishing, ISBN 9781739484569

Additional details of Mel Croucher's work are available on the Wikipedia page: https://en.wikipedia.org/wiki/Mel_Croucher

Also Available from Extremis Publishing

# DIGITAL PIONEER SPIRIT

## The Freewheeling Creative Innovation of Mel Croucher on the Home Microcomputer

## By Thomas A. Christie

Get ready to step into the revolutionary world of Mel Croucher – a genuine maverick who redefined the digital age. In *Digital Pioneer Spirit*, Thomas A. Christie unravels the extraordinary career of the man who blazed a trail as Britain's first multimedia personality.

Mel Croucher was a virtuoso talent even in an age of innovators. From his ground-breaking computer games like *PiMania*, *iD*, and *Deus Ex Machina* – a cult classic that fused gaming, art, and music – to his razor-sharp journalism and visionary writing, Croucher's work shattered boundaries and challenged conventions. A counter-cultural genius with a boundlessly whimsical sense of humour, he stood as an iconoclast in the earliest days of the home computer industry, harnessing emerging technology to inspire, provoke, and entertain.

With meticulous research, Christie paints a compelling portrait of a creative rebel whose influence still ripples through today's digital culture. Whether you're a tech enthusiast, a gaming historian, or an admirer of unconventional minds, *Digital Pioneer Spirit* is an unmissable exploration of the man who turned bits and bytes into a bold new art form.

Discover the amazing true story of Mel Croucher – a digital pioneer, a cultural provocateur, and a true original.

For details of new and forthcoming books from Extremis Publishing, including our monthly podcasts and regular newsletter please visit our official website at:

**www.extremispublishing.com**

or follow us on social media at:

www.facebook.com/extremispublishing

www.linkedin.com/company/extremis-publishing-ltd-/